Y0-BQN-380

George H. Shen

The New Birth

THE NEW BIRTH

John Wesley

A Modern English Edition
by Thomas C. Oden

1817

Harper & Row, Publishers, San Francisco
Cambridge, Hagerstown, New York, Philadelphia
London, Mexico City, São Paulo, Sydney

Biblical quotations, unless otherwise noted, are from the *New English Bible,*
© The Delegates of the Oxford University Press and The Syndics of the
Cambridge University Press, 1961, 1972. Reprinted by permission

THE NEW BIRTH. Copyright © 1984 by Thomas C. Oden. All rights
reserved. Printed in the United States of America. No part of this book
may be used or reproduced in any manner whatsoever without written
permission except in the case of brief quotations embodied in critical
articles and reviews. For information address Harper & Row, Publishers,
Inc., 10 East 53rd Street, New York, NY 10022. Published simultaneously
in Canada by Fitzhenry & Whiteside, Limited, Toronto.

FIRST EDITION

Designed by Catherine Hopkins

Library of Congress Cataloging in Publication Data

Wesley, John 1703–1791.
  THE NEW BIRTH

  Contents: Introduction — The new birth — The first fruits of spirit —
[etc.]
  1. Methodist Church—Sermons. 2. Sermons, English. I. Oden,
Thomas C. II. Title.
BX8333.W418N48   1984   252'.07   83–48460
ISBN 0–06–069312–6

84 85 86 87 88   10 9 8 7 6 5 4 3 2 1

Contents

- INTRODUCTION -

By Thomas C. Oden

Here are five of the most widely read meditations in Christian history. They have changed lives. Now they are available in modern English.

Nicodemus asked of Jesus: "Can one be born again?" The same question is being asked today. This book leads us through major scriptural themes to make clear that promise of new birth in Christ. Twentieth-century readers will find these meditations as valuable as did others over two hundred years ago, when Wesley wrote them.

Who was John Wesley? Founder of the Methodist movement and the Wesleyan family of churches, his life spanned most of the eighteenth century (1703–1791). While studying at Oxford, he gathered together a group of earnest, devout, and scholarly Christians, who became known as "Bible Moths," "The Holy Club"—or the nickname that finally stuck, "Methodists." They searched the Scriptures, visited the sick, poor, and imprisoned, and sought to lead a life of scriptural holiness. In 1735 Wesley set out on a mission to the Indians and colonists of Georgia, but his preaching, especially against the slave-trade, gin, and lax pastoral practice, alienated him from his congregation. By 1738 he had returned to England, wistfully musing that "I went to America to convert the Indians; but, oh, who shall convert me?"

On May 24, 1738, in a meeting on Aldersgate Street in London, Wesley found his heart "strangely warmed" as he listened to a reading of Luther's *Preface to Romans.* Wesley began to preach the new birth in parish churches and to small groups of believers. Finally, finding the churches closed to him, he began field-preaching to the Kingswood coalminers in 1739, and from there he preached all over England. To sustain Christians in their new life in Christ, Wesley formed societies everywhere he preached. From the London-Bristol-Newcastle triangle, he later extended his mission to Ireland, Scotland, Wales, and North America.

With the exception of the last of these meditations, everything in this collection comes from the early period of Wesley's preaching, 1739–1745. They reveal a person of deep scriptural wisdom, broad learning, tolerance, and charity. Wesley sought to ground the expanding revival in solid scriptural teaching. During this period he turned frequently to those key texts on the new birth: John 3, Romans 8, and 1 John 3–5. These sermons remain classics two centuries later. They have been through two dozen editions in as many decades and have been read by millions on every continent. They have helped countless persons come to know Christ better and follow his call.

Although Wesley's sermons continue to be studied by theological experts, they were from the beginning intended for popular, general audiences. Yet modern readers encounter certain difficulties as they try to read Wesley. The obstacles lie not in the content of Wesley's message, but in the old-fashioned language that encases it. The proper, tightly woven, Augustan English, although beautiful in its own way, is growing more and more distant from our common speech. It is that language gap that I am trying to overcome in this modern language edition.

An energetic family of movements, missions, churches, and ministries has emerged from the preaching of Wesley on the new birth and from the work of the Spirit witnessed to in these discourses. As son of an Anglican minister, Wesley was ordained an Anglican and was a frequent defender of Anglican teaching and practice. It is surprising to survey the range of world-wide church bodies that continue to look to Wesley for their basic orientation to Christian faith: the United Methodist Church, the Salvation Army, the African Methodist Episcopal Zion Church, the Free Methodist Church, the Church of the Nazarene, the Wesleyan Church, the Methodist Churches of Great Britain and Ireland, and many autonomous Methodist Churches around the world.

But Wesley's spiritual legacy goes far beyond structural bounds. It is seen in the diffuse spreading of various holiness movements, pentecostal, camp meeting, and other charismatic movements that have reached into virtually every corner of Protestantism. Many Wesleyan themes also resonate deeply with much current Catholic spirituality. The central cluster of Wesleyan teachings—heart ecumenism, the trustworthiness of Scripture, the intimate relation of Christ's work for us and the Spirit's work in us, the new birth, nurturant communities of self-disclosure, scriptural holiness, and the gifts of the Spirit—are now infused into many strains of the Christian tradition.

Many who know a little about Wesley wish to know more. Many know a stray quote here or there, but few lay persons have been given a chance to feel the direct power of his teaching by reading him firsthand in current English. Yet Wesley seems to be available only in massive packages. The fourteen-volume Thomas Jackson third edition of 1831 is still being reprinted. The scholarly, multivolume Bicentennial edition will in time be available. The ordinary reader, however, has no obvious place to begin in such a vast outlay of documents, and many have expressed a hope for a modest book encompassing Wesley's best writings in an unpretentious form.

One of my motives is to render Wesley available to modern readers in sexually inclusive language. Although some may object, most, I believe, will affirm the effort at fairness, especially in the case of a Christian teacher whose mission depended so profoundly upon the ministry of women. I have other purposes, however, although that alone could justify the effort. I have tried to state Wesley's meanings in vital, straightforward, modern prose, without losing any of the energy of Wesley's original text. I have deliberately updated words like *shouldst, wanteth not, tres-*

passeth, wheresoever, thereof, and *thine.* Although these words were completely familiar to Wesley's original audience, they now make the text read like an obstacle course. I do not change Wesley's meaning by changing such archaic words.

There are two ways a reader may be helped to move through this language barrier. One is to offer detailed footnotes that explain problems of meaning and opaque allusions at each step along the way. Another —and for our purposes, a better—way is through a dynamic equivalency rendition of the text: that is, rendering meanings carefully, but without being locked into the original syntax or literal form. The annotative method preserves the text faithfully with detailed scholarly comment; the dynamic equivalency method, developed largely by contemporary Bible translators, renders the text more directly accessible to a wider audience. This method bears little resemblance to the paraphrase, in which large portions may be omitted in the interest of condensation. (On the contrary, wherever I have omitted a phrase, I have inserted ellipses.)

The dynamic equivalency method has been widely used in English literature. Fine literary editions of works by Geoffrey Chaucer, Piers Plowman, Thomas More, Edmund Spenser, John Donne, Thomas Hobbes, John Milton, John Bunyan, Richard Baxter, and Robert Burns have all appeared in slightly or greatly amended renderings of their original form, in order to make them more available to the current readers. This procedure is not unique; however, fewer religious than literary figures have been presented in this way.

The purpose of this book is quite different from that of the excellent four-volume edition of *Wesley's Sermons,* edited by my principal mentor, Albert C. Outler. Those are richly endowed volumes that scholarly readers will study with joy. This small book fills an entirely different niche. Outler seeks to deliver accurately the best eighteenth-century text without any omissions or changes and to offer a substantial commentary on the text—its allusions, historical sources, problems, and ambiguities. This book focuses on a single theme central to Wesley's teaching, the New Birth, and presents in vital, readable words for today's lay audience his five best writings that develop that theme.

As a Scripture scholar, Wesley was well-versed in Greek and Hebrew and often referred his hearer to the original Greek and Hebrew terms. In his sermons he used the familiar King James Version. As I began to work on this book, I decided that Wesley's frequent scriptural allusions and references should be presented in some modern English version. Why? Because Wesley's message is addressed not only to his eighteenth-century audience but also to that of the twentieth century. After much reflection, I chose for this purpose the New English Bible, an admirable modern product of Wesley's own Anglican tradition. I believe that Wesley would not have objected, for he himself set the precedent by using the best available text of his time.

My rule has been to limit changes only to those that most accurately express and sustain the original meaning or intended nuance of Wesley's text, not to add any meaning or attribution of my own. Wherever I have rendered an older or dated phrase into words that more clearly connect with our time, I appeal (as did Wesley) to the root meaning of the term stated in plain terms. (I have added headings, to provide a clearer picture of the structure and development of the discourse.) I have tried to state clearly and accurately the meaning of Wesley's original text in words and forms that are easily understandable in standard, everyday English. My intent is to give the reader maximum understanding of the content of Wesley's text.

I am sympathetic with those who for sentiment or other reasons hesitate to change Wesley's late Augustan style of Hanoverian English to modern English. But it is pertinent to ask this test-case question: Would you translate the German Reformer Martin Luther into sixteenth-century English or modern English? If you say modern, then what should prevent us from applying the same principle in rendering Wesley's antiquated English into modern English?

Each sermon is followed by one of John Wesley's prayers and the text of a hymn by Charles Wesley. They offer a moving glimpse of the vital religious context in which the sermons were written and to which they were originally addressed. The prayers and hymns remind us that Wesley's sermons ordinarily were delivered to a living community of prayer, celebration, intentional behavioral change, and social service. Charles Wesley, younger brother of John, was an original founder of the "Holy Club" and also a Georgia missionary. Charles was one of the most gifted and prolific of all English hymnwriters, authoring some 7,270 hymns, including many that continue to be favorites today and are found in the hymnals of a variety of denominations. These hymns reflect the heart of Wesleyan spirituality and their texts are appropriate for meditative reading.

—T. C. O.
Drew University
United Methodist Archives Center
Madison, New Jersey

· ONE ·

The New Birth

You must be born over again. (John 3:7)

If any teachings within the whole compass of Christianity may be properly termed "fundamental," they are doubtless these two—justification and the new birth. Justification speaks of that great work which God does *for* us in forgiving our sins. The new birth speaks of the great work which God does *in* us in renewing our fallen nature.

Chronologically, neither one necessarily comes before the other. For when we are justified by the grace of God through the redemption that is in Jesus, we are also "born from spirit" (John 3:8). But as a matter of orderly *thinking,* justification is prior to the new birth. For we first become aware that God's anger has been turned away, and then that God's Spirit is working in our hearts.

How incomparably important then it must be to everyone clearly to understand these fundamental teachings! Out of deep conviction many excellent writers have dealt with justification in fine detail, explaining every point related to it and fully opening the Scriptures which illumine it. Similarly, many have written about the new birth, and some fairly exhaustively, yet not as clearly as might have been desired, nor as deeply and accurately. They have either given a dark, abstruse account of it, or a slight and superficial one. Therefore a full, and at the same time clear, account of the new birth still seems to be needed. Such an account must try to give a satisfactory answer to these three questions:

First, why must we be born again? What is the foundation of this teaching of the new birth?

Second, how are we to be born again? What is the nature of the new birth?

Third, to what purpose must we be born again? To what end is it necessary?

With the help of God I shall briefly and plainly answer these questions and then add some remarks that follow naturally from them.

Why Rebirth Is Needed

Why must we be born again? What is the foundation of this teaching?

1. Humanity Created in God's Image

The foundation is sunk as deeply as the creation of the world. In the scriptural account of creation we read that the triune God said, " 'Let us make man in our image and likeness' " (Gen. 1:26). "So God created man in his own image; in the image of God he created him; male and female he created them" (Gen. 1:27).

It is not only in God's *natural image* that humanity is made, as a reflection of God's own immortality, as a spiritual being, endowed with understanding, freedom of will, and various affections. Nor is humanity created simply in God's *political image,* as governor of this earthly sphere, able to "rule over the fish in the sea, the birds of heaven, and every living thing that moves upon the earth" (Gen. 1:28). Above all, humanity is made in God's *moral image,* which, according to the Apostle, "shows itself in the just and devout life called for by the truth" (Eph. 4:24). Humanity was from the beginning fashioned in this natural, political, and moral image of God.

2. Created "Very Good"

"God is love" (1 John 4:9). If so, then man and woman in their original creation were full of love; love was the sole principle of all their tempers, thoughts, words, and actions. God is full of justice, mercy, and truth. So were human beings originally as they came from the hands of their Creator. God is spotless purity. So was humanity in the beginning pure from every sinful blot. Otherwise God could not have pronounced humanity, as well as all the other works of God's hands, "very good" (Gen. 1:31). This blessing could not have been made if human creation had been blighted by sin, lacking righteousness and true holiness. There is no way to evade the point: If we suppose that an intelligent creature does not love God and is neither righteous nor holy, then we necessarily suppose that the creature can hardly be pronounced good, and certainly not "very good."

3. Able to Stand, Liable to Fall

But, although human beings are made in the image of God, they are not made to be fixed and unchangeable. This would have been inconsistent with that state of trial in which God had decided to place them. They were, therefore, created able to stand and yet liable to fall.

God himself called their attention to this vulnerability and gave them a solemn warning concerning it. Nevertheless, mankind did not remain faithful, but fell from this original righteousness, having eaten from the tree that God had forbidden (Gen. 3:11). By this willful act of disobedience to their Creator, this flat rebellion against their Sovereign, they openly declared that they would no longer have God to guide them, but rather they would be governed strictly by their own will. They decided that they would be ruled not by the will of God who created them, nor seek their happiness in God, but rather from the world and the works of their own hands. God had warned them previously, "For on the day that you eat from it, you will certainly die" (Gen. 2:17), a divine command that could not be broken.

4. Spiritual Death

The moment they broke God's command, they died, died to God—the most dreadful of all deaths.

They lost the life of companionship with God: they were separated from God, in union with whom their spiritual life consisted.

As the body dies when it is separated from the soul, the soul dies when it is separated from God. This is what happened to Adam and Eve on the day, the hour, they ate of the forbidden fruit. And they immediately gave proof of this separation by showing by their behavior that the love of God was extinguished in their soul; and they were now to live as "strangers to the life that is in God" (Eph. 4:18).

5. Loss of the Moral Image of God

Instead of trusting God, they now felt the servile power of fear. They fled from the presence of the Lord. So little did they retain even a basic knowledge of God or remember that God fills the heaven and earth, that they tried to hide "from the Lord God among the trees of the garden" (Gen. 3:8). This shows how deeply they had lost both the knowledge and the love of God, without which the image of God could not remain vital.

In being deprived of the moral image of God, they became unholy as well as unhappy. In the void left by this, they sank further into pride and self-will—reflecting more the image of the devil than God—and into sensual appetites and desires, the image of the beasts that perish.

The phrase "on the day that you eat from it, you will certainly die" is thought by some to refer to temporal death and that alone—the death of the body only. The answer is plain: to take this interpretation is flatly and palpably to make God a liar, to suggest that the God of truth could positively affirm something contrary to truth. For in fact Adam did not even *die* in that particular bodily sense "on the day that [he ate] from it." He lived on, resisting temporal death, for a very long time —Scripture says for over nine hundred years (Gen. 5:5). So this warning cannot possibly be understood to refer to the death of the body without impeaching the veracity of God. It must, therefore, be understood as referring to spiritual death—the loss of the life and the image of God.

6. We Follow Adam

This is the sense in which in Adam's death all humankind died. The fall encompasses all human beings who were yet to come from Adam. The natural consequence of this is that everyone who follows after Adam comes into the world spiritually dead—dead to God, wholly dead in sin, entirely void of the life of God, lacking the moral image of God and of all that righteousness and holiness in which Adam originally was created. Instead of this, all of us born into the world now mirror the power of sin in our pride and self-will. We seem like beasts in our sensual appetites and desires.

This, then, is why new birth is required. Our entire nature has become corrupted. It is precisely because we have been born into a sinful world that we now must be "born again." This is why everyone that is born of woman must be born of the Spirit of God.

The Meaning of the New Birth

But how is one to be born again? What is the nature of the new birth? This is our second question, a question of the highest conceivable order of importance. In so weighty a concern, we ought not to be content with a slight inquiry, but must examine it with all possible care. We must ponder it in our hearts, until we fully understand this crucial point and clearly see how we are to be born again.

We are not expecting here to develop a minute, philosophical account of how this is done. Our Lord sufficiently guards us against any such expectation in the words immediately following our text, when he reminds Nicodemus of a fact as indisputable as any in the whole compass of nature, yet one which the wisest one under the sun is not able fully to explain: "The wind blows where it wills"—not by your power or wisdom; "You hear the sound of it"—you are absolutely assured, beyond all doubt, that it blows; "but you do not know where it comes from, or where it is going"—the precise manner of how it begins and ends, rises and falls, no one can tell; "So with everyone who is born from spirit" (John 3:8)! You may be absolutely assured that something exists, just as you are of the wind when it blows, but the precise manner of its action—in this case how the Holy Spirit works in the soul—neither you nor the wisest will be able to explain. Without descending into curious, critical inquiries, it is sufficient for the purposes of rational Christian discourse that we offer a plain scriptural account of the nature of the new birth that will satisfy any reasonable person who desires salvation.

1. Adoption into the Family of God

The expression "being born again" was not first used by our Lord in his conversation with Nicodemus. It was well known before that time and was in common use among the Jews when our Savior appeared among them. When an adult nonbeliever was convinced that the Jewish religion was of God and desired to be a part of it, it was the custom then to baptize him first before he was admitted to circumcision. It was when he was baptized that he was said to be "born again," by which it was meant that one who had been a child of darkness was now adopted into the family of God and accounted one of God's own children. As a "teacher of Israel," (John 3:10) Nicodemus must have understood this expression well. But our Lord uses it in a stronger sense than that to which Nicodemus was accustomed, and this might be the reason for his asking, "How is this possible?" (John 3:9).

2. The Analogy of Birth

The new birth cannot be taken literally. No one can physically "enter his mother's womb a second time and be born" (John 3:4). But it may occur spiritually. One may be born from above, born of God, born of the Spirit, in a manner which bears a very near analogy to the natural birth.

Before a child is born into the world doesn't he have eyes, but does not see? Doesn't he have ears, but does not hear? He has a very imperfect use of the other senses. He has no knowledge of any of the things of the world, nor any natural understanding. We do not call this embryonic existence in the full sense "birth"; only when the cord is cut do we say that the child properly is "born" and "begins to live." But as soon as the child is born, he begins to breathe and live in a wholly different way than before. He begins to see the light and to recognize various objects around him. Hearing is activated, and he hears different sounds striking his ears. All the other organs of sense begin to work in their own spheres.

Listen to the profound analogy at work here! While we are in a mere natural state, before we are born of God, we have, in a spiritual sense, the rudiments of eyes, but see nothing. It is as if a thick, impenetrable veil were pulled over them. We have ears, but we hear nothing; and we are most deaf precisely to that which we most need to hear. Our other spiritual senses are all locked up. We are in the same condition as if we did not even have them. Therefore, we are without knowledge of God, are not in communication with God, are not at all acquainted with God. We have no reliable knowledge of the things of God, of the Spirit and eternity. Though one is a living person, one is not yet alive as a Christian.

3. The Awakening of Spiritual Senses

As soon as one is born of God, there is a total change in all these ways. "I pray that your inward eyes may be illumined" says Paul (Eph. 1:18). The One of old who commanded: " 'Out of darkness let light shine,' has caused his light to shine within us, to give the light of revelation—the revelation of the glory of God in the face of Jesus Christ" (2 Cor. 4:2). Similarly, our ears are opened, and we are now capable of hearing the inward voice of God saying, "Take heart, my Son; your sins are forgiven" (Matt. 9:2). "You may go; do not sin again" (John 8:11). In this way God speaks to our hearts, though perhaps not in these very words. We are now ready to hear whatever the Spirit, as teacher, is willing from time to time to reveal to us. We "feel in our hearts," to use the language of the Anglican "Homily on Rogation Week," "the mighty working of the Spirit of God."

This mighty spiritual transformation is not to be understood in a common, hedonistic sense, as worldly minds have stupidly and willfully misunderstood the expression even when it is repeatedly explained otherwise. We mean neither more nor less than this: Believers feel, and are inwardly sensible of, the gifts which the Spirit of God is eliciting in their hearts. They feel, and are conscious of, a "peace of God, which is beyond our utmost understanding" (Phil. 4:7) and are "transported with a joy too great for words" (1 Pet. 1:8). "Such a hope is no mockery, because God's love has flooded our inmost heart through the Holy Spirit he has given us" (Rom. 5:5). Thus, they are able to exercise all their spiritual senses to discern spiritual good and evil. By the use of these senses, they daily increase in the knowledge of God, of Jesus Christ whom God has sent, and of everything pertaining to his inward kingdom.

4. New Life in Christ

Such a person may be properly said to be alive; God having awakened him by his Spirit, he is alive to God through Jesus Christ. He lives a life the world does not understand, a life that "lies hidden with Christ in God" (Col. 3:3). God is continually breathing life into the soul, and the soul is returning the breath of life to God. Grace is descending into his heart, while his prayer and praise ascend to heaven. By this communion between God and the person, this fellowship with the Father and the Son, as by a kind of spiritual respiration, the life of God in the soul is sustained. In this way the children of God grow up until they attain to a maturity "measured by nothing less than the full stature of Christ" (Eph. 4:13).

At this point we can state plainly the essential nature of the new birth. It is the great change that God works in the soul when he brings it into life, when he raises it from the death of sin to the life of righteousness. It is the change made in the whole soul by the almighty Spirit of God when it is "created in Christ Jesus" (Eph. 2:10); when it is "made new in mind and spirit," having "put on the new nature of God's creating, which shows itself in the just and devout life called for by the truth" (Eph. 4:24); when the love of the world is changed into the love of God, pride into humility, passion into meekness, hatred and malice into a sincere, tender, disinterested love for all mankind. In a word, it is that change in which the earthly, sensual, demeaned mind is transformed into the mind which was in Christ Jesus (Phil. 2:5). This is the nature of the new birth. So it is "with everyone who is born from spirit" (John 3:8).

The Necessity of New Birth

It is not difficult for anyone who has considered these things, therefore, to see the necessity of the new birth. This is our third question: To what end is it necessary that we should be born again?

It is very easily discerned that a new birth is required if we are to share in God's holiness. For what is the holy life, according to Scripture? Not a bare external religion or round of outward duties, no matter how many they may be or how exactly performed.

No. Gospel holiness is no less than the image of God stamped upon the heart. It is nothing other than having that mind which was in Christ Jesus. In it all gracious affections and tempers are mingled together. It implies such a continual, thankful love for God who has not withheld from us his Son, his only Son, that it becomes natural, and in some way necessary to us, to love every human being. It fills us with "compassion, kindness, humility, gentleness, patience" (Col. 3:12). . . .

Unless one is born again, one cannot be happy in this world. For it is not possible, in the nature of things, that someone can become truly happy who is not holy. Even the poor ungodly poet Juvenal could tell us that "no bad man can be happy" (Satires, IV, 8). The reason is plain: all unholy temperaments are uneasy temperaments. I speak not only of the volatile passions such as malice, hatred, envy, jealousy, and revenge. They create enough of a present hell in our hearts. I speak also of the softer passions, which may give a thousand times more pain than pleasure if not kept within due bounds. Even "hope," when "deferred" (and how often must this be the case!), "makes the heart sick" (Prov. 13:12).

Every desire which is not in harmony with the will of God is liable to cause us to "spike" ourselves "on many thorny griefs" (1 Tim. 6:10). All those general sources of sin—pride, self-will, and idolatry—are, in the same proportion as they prevail, general sources of misery. So as long as these take command of any person, happiness has no room. But they will continue to be in command until the bent of our nature is changed —that is, until we are born again. This is another reason why new birth is so absolutely necessary: It is the surest basis of happiness in this world, as well as in the world to come.

Consequences of New Birth

Finally I will add a few inferences that follow naturally from these observations. It follows that baptism is not the new birth. They are not the same. Many, indeed, seem to imagine that they are; or at least they speak as if they thought so, even though this opinion is not publicly avowed by any traditional Christian confession whatever, certainly none in this country, either by the established Church or those dissenting from it. The judgment of the Reformed tradition is clearly declared in the Large Catechism of the Westminster Assembly: "The parts of a sacrament are two: the one an outward and sensible sign; the other, an inward and spiritual grace thereby signified. . . . Baptism is a sacrament wherein Christ hath ordained the washing with water, to be a sign and seal of regeneration by His Spirit." Here it is clear that baptism, the sign, is sharply distinguished from new birth, the thing signified.

In the Anglican Catechism, the distinction is stated with utmost clarity. What is a sacrament? "An outward and visible sign of an inward and spiritual grace." What is the outward aspect of baptism? "Water, in which the person is baptized, in the name of the Father, Son, and Holy Ghost." What is the inward part, the thing signified? "A death unto sin, and a new birth unto righteousness." Nothing is plainer, according to the Church of England, than that baptism is distinguishable from the new birth.

The reasoning underlying this is so clear and evident that we hardly need to cite other authorities. For what can be more plain than that water is an outward and visible thing, while the new birth is hidden and internal? They are completely distinguishable. One is an outwardly visible act of cleansing the body. The other is an inward change worked by God in the soul. One is as distinguishable from the other as the soul is from the body or water from the Holy Spirit.

As new birth is distinguishable from baptism, so it does not always accompany baptism. They do not constantly go together. One may possibly be "born from water" (John 3:5) yet not be "born from Spirit" (John 3:8). Sometimes there may be the outward sign where there is not yet the inward grace. . . .

The new birth is a part of sanctification, not the whole. It is the gate to it, the entrance into it. When we are born again, then our sanctification, our inward and outward holiness begins. After that we are enabled gradually to "speak the truth in love; so shall we fully grow up into Christ. He is the head and on him the whole body depends." (Eph. 4:15, 16). This expression of the Apostle admirably shows the difference between new birth and sanctification, by means of an analogy between natural and spiritual things. We might speak of the moment of birth as an instant, or at least a very short time. After that it takes a long time for the child gradually and slowly to grow, until the child reaches the stature of an adult. Similarly, a child is born of God in a short time, if not in a moment, but it is by slow degrees that the child afterward grows up to the measure of the full stature of Christ. The same relation, therefore, that exists between our natural birth and our growth, also exists between our new birth and our sanctification.

A final point of such great importance that it deserves more lengthy consideration is: What can we say to one who willfully continues in sin? If we love the souls of persons around us, what can we say to one who persists in drunkenness and Sabbath-breaking? If we are grieved to think of their spiritual death, can we withhold from them the witness: "You must be born again"? Some may answer: "You cannot talk to me that way. It is quite uncharitable. Haven't I already been baptized? I cannot be born again now!" Even if you are as old as Nicodemus was, still: "In truth, in very truth I tell you, unless a man has been born over again he cannot see the kingdom of God" (John 3:3). One cannot be saved who cannot be born again. Who then is uncharitable? One who says flatly that you cannot be born again? No, it is more charitable to say that one may be born again and so become an heir of salvation. One who says absolutely, "You cannot be born again," tends to block the way to salvation, to show the way to hell, and all this in the name of charity.

But perhaps the sinner to whom in real charity we

say, "You must be born again," has been taught to say, "I reject the whole idea; for I do not need to be born again, since I was born again when I was baptized. What! Would you have me deny my baptism?" I answer: There is nothing under heaven that can excuse a lie. Were the person an open sinner, I would say: If you have been baptized, you are not owning it. How greatly does this aggravate your guilt and your alienation from God! You were devoted to God when you were eight days old, but you have spent all these years devoting yourself to the power of evil. . . . Look at yourself candidly. Do love of the world, pride, anger, lust, foolish desire, and a whole train of twisted affections stand in your life where they should not? Have you allowed all these plagues to enter into your soul, which was once a temple of the Holy Spirit, set apart as "a spiritual dwelling for God" (Eph. 2:22) and solemnly dedicated to God? And will you take pride in this, you who once belonged to God? O be ashamed! blush! hide yourself in a hole somewhere! Do not gloat about what ought to fill you with remorse and make you ashamed before God and humanity!

I answer plainly that you have already denied your baptism, and done it in the most effective way. You have denied it a thousand times a thousand times, and you do so still, day by day. For in your baptism you renounced the devil and all his works. Any time you give space for him again in your life, you deny your baptism. Therefore, you deny it by every willful sin; by every act of rottenness, insobriety, or revenge; by every obscene or profane word that comes out of your mouth. Every time you profane the day of the Lord, you thereby deny your baptism. Moreover, every time you do anything to another that you would not wish to have others do to you, your baptism has been forgotten.

Whether baptized or unbaptized, you must be born again. Without rebirth there is no beginning for the life of inward holiness; and without inward as well as outward holiness, you cannot be happy, even in this world, much less in the world to come.

Now you will say to me: "But I do no harm to anyone! I am honest and just in all my dealings; I do not curse or take the Lord's name in vain; I do not profane the Lord's day; I am no drunkard; I do not slander my neighbor, or live in any willful sin." If this is so, we can only wish that everyone had come as far as you have come. But you must go farther yet, or you cannot be saved, for still "you must be born over again." Do you add, "I do go farther yet; for I not only do no harm, but do all the good I can"? Really? All the good? Possible? I fear you have had a thousand opportunities for doing good which you have permitted to pass by unimproved, and for which, therefore, you are accountable to God. But if you had improved them all, if you really had done all the good you possibly could to all, yet this does not in any way alter the case. Still "you must be born over again." Without this, nothing will do any good finally for the sin and corruption in your impoverished soul. "But I constantly attend all the ordinances of God: I keep to my church and sacrament." You do well, but all this will not save you except you be born again. Go to church twice a day; go to the Lord's table every week; say ever so many prayers in private; hear ever so many good sermons; read ever so many good books; still "you must be born over again." None of these will finally take the place of the new birth. Nothing can.

Let this be your continual prayer, if you have not already experienced this inward change worked by God: "Lord, add this to all your blessings—let me be born again! Deny whatever you will, but do not deny this—let me be born from above! Take away whatever you view as an obstacle to this—reputation, fortune, friends, health—only give me this, to be born of the Spirit, to be received among the children of God! Let me be born, "not of mortal parentage but of immortal, through the living and enduring word of God" (1 Pet. 1:23), and then let me daily "grow in the grace and in the knowledge of our Lord and Saviour Jesus Christ" (2 Pet. 3:18)!

O Lord, help; O Lord, save; O Lord, deliver me. Teach me the truth as it is in Jesus. Save me from my own self-will, and let thy will be done in me and by me. O make me thy child by adoption and grace. Renew me daily with thy Holy Spirit, and guide me in all my ways, until thou hast perfected me for thy heavenly kingdom. Amen. (*WJW* XI, 271)

Come, Holy Ghost, our hearts inspire.
Let us Thine influence prove:
Source of the old prophetic fire,
Fountain of life and love.

Come, Holy Ghost, for moved by Thee
The prophets wrote and spoke
Unlock the truth, thyself the Key;
Unseal the sacred Book.

Expand Thy wings, celestial Dove;
Brood o'er our nature's night.
On our discovered spirits move,
And let there now be light.

God, through himself, we then shall know,
If Thou within us shine,
And sound, with all Thy saints below,
The depths of love divine.

(*WH* 125)

- TWO -

The Firstfruits of the Spirit

There is no condemnation for those who are united with Christ Jesus, because in Christ Jesus the life-giving law of the Spirit has set you free from the law of sin and death. (Rom. 8:1, 2)

By "those who are united with Christ Jesus," Paul evidently means those who truly believe in Christ, who having been "justified through faith" "continue at peace with God through our Lord Jesus Christ" (Rom. 5:1). Those who trust God in this way have been set "free from the law of sin and death" and no longer follow the impulses of corrupted nature, but rather "walk . . . after the Spirit" (Rom. 8:1, KJV). Their thoughts, words, and actions are under the guidance of the blessed Spirit of God.

This is why there is "no condemnation" for them. Primarily there is no condemnation from God, since they "are justified by God's free grace alone, through his act of liberation in the person of Christ Jesus" (Rom. 3:24). God has forgiven all their iniquities and blotted out all their sins.

Furthermore, there is no condemnation from within themselves. For "this is the Spirit that we have received from God and not the spirit of the world, so that we may know all that God of his own grace has given us" (1 Cor. 2:12). "In that cry the Spirit of God joins with our spirit in testifying that we are God's children" (Rom. 8:16). To this we add the testimony of our own conscience which "assures us that in our dealings with our fellow-men, and above all in our dealings with you, our conduct has been governed by a devout and godly sincerity, by the grace of God and not by worldly wisdom" (2 Cor. 1:12).

But regrettably this text on "no condemnation" has been frequently misunderstood, and misunderstood in a dangerous way. Many who tend to be "ignorant and unstable" (the Greek word implies those who are untaught of God and, consequently, not established in the truth that follows after godliness) have misinterpreted it "to their own ruin" (2 Pet. 3:16), so I propose to ask, as clearly as I can:

Who are "those who are united with Christ Jesus" who "do not walk after the flesh, but after the Spirit"?

In what sense do they now experience "no condemnation"?

What practical consequences follow?

Life in Christ

Who are "in Christ"? Aren't they those who believe in Jesus Christ? Those who have found themselves "incorporated in him" with no righteousness of their own? Those who live by "the righteousness which comes from faith in Christ, given by God in response to faith" (Phil. 3:9)?

They are properly said to be "in Christ" whose "release is secured" and whose "sins are forgiven" (Col. 1:14). They live in Christ, and Christ lives in them. They are joined to the Lord in one Spirit. They are grafted into Christ, as branches into the vine. As bodily members are related to the brain in ways that go far beyond our precise description, so are Christian believers united with Christ. Words can never fully express this coherence.

No one who "dwells in him is a sinner" (1 John 3:6). Our "conduct, no longer under the control of our lower nature, is directed by the Spirit" (Rom. 8:4). "Flesh," in Paul's usage, means corrupt nature. Paul thought that anyone could recognize "the kind of behaviour that belongs to the lower nature" (Gal. 5:19). But "if you are guided by the Spirit you will not fulfil the desires of your lower nature" (Gal. 5:16). Those who walk by the Spirit are not tyrannized by the lower nature. "That nature sets its desires against the Spirit, while the Spirit fights against it. They are in conflict with one another so that what you will you cannot do" (Gal. 5:17).

The original Greek should not be translated flatly that you cannot in any sense "do what you will," for Paul would never be found arguing that the flesh is completely victorious over the Spirit. That would assert just the reverse of what Paul was seeking to demonstrate. Such a rendering has little to do with the original text of the Apostle. Rather, those who are "in Christ" have "crucified the lower nature with its passions and desires" (Gal. 5:24). They abstain from "the kind of behaviour that belongs to the lower nature: fornication, impurity, and indecency; idolatry and sorcery; quarrels, a contentious temper, envy, fits of rage, selfish ambitions, dissensions, party intrigues, and jealousies; drinking bouts, orgies, and the like" (Gal. 5:19); that is, from every conception, word, and work to which the corruption of nature tends to lead.

Although they may feel the root of bitterness remaining in themselves, they are nevertheless endued with power from on high to trample it continually under foot, so that it cannot, like a "noxious weed," grow up to "poison the whole" (Heb. 12:15). Every assault which they undergo only gives them fresh occasion to praise, to cry out, "God be praised, he gives us the victory through our Lord Jesus Christ" (1 Cor. 15:57).

They now walk according to the Spirit, both in their hearts and lives. They are taught by Christ to love God and their neighbor with a love that is like "an inner spring always welling up for eternal life" (John 4:14). By Christ they are led steadily toward every holy desire, every godly affection and temperament, until every thought which arises in their heart is finally grounded in God's holiness.

Those who walk in the Spirit are also led by Christ into personal conversation that reflects God's holiness. Their speech is "always gracious, and never insipid" (Col. 4:6), seasoned with the love of God and reverence for God. "No bad language must pass your lips, but only what is good and helpful to the occasion, so that it brings a blessing to those who hear it" (Eph. 4:29). In this way they exercise themselves daily, doing what is pleasing to God. In their outward behavior they seek to follow Christ, who left an example that we might "follow in his steps" (1 Pet. 2:21). In their meeting with their neighbor, they daily exercise their ability to walk in justice, mercy, and truth. "Whatever you are doing," in every circumstance of life, "do all for the honour of God" (1 Cor. 10:31). Such are those who indeed walk according to the Spirit. Filled with faith and the Spirit, they receive in their hearts and show forth in their lives, in the whole course of their words and actions, the genuine fruits of the Spirit of God.

What are the fruits of the Spirit? "Love, joy, peace, patience, kindness, goodness, fidelity, gentleness, and self-control" (Gal. 5:22), and whatever else is lovely or worthy of praise. "In all such ways they will add lustre to the doctrine of God our Saviour" (Titus 2:10). In these ways they demonstrate clearly to all that they are indeed made active by the same Spirit that "raised Jesus our Lord from the dead" (Rom. 4:24).

Without Condemnation

My next purpose is to clarify the sense in which there is now "no condemnation for those who are united with Christ Jesus" (Rom. 8:1)—who are not tyrannized by their lower natures, but who walk according to the Spirit.

1. Past Sins Are Not Remembered

To believers in Christ who walk in this way, there is "no condemnation" for their past sins. God does not condemn their past. It is as though these past sins had never been, as if a stone were thrown to the bottom of the sea. God does not recall them at all any more! For God sent Christ "to be the means of expiating sin by his sacrificial death, effective through faith. God meant by this to demonstrate his justice, because in his forbearance he had overlooked the sins of the past" (Rom. 3:25, 26). Nothing is charged to their account. Even the memory of sin has perished.

As a result, there is now no condemnation in their own hearts over past sin. There is no remaining inward sense of guilt or latent dread of the righteous anger of God. For they now have a reliable witness in themselves, aware of what has happened on their behalf in the sacrifice of Christ. "The Spirit you have received is not a spirit of slavery leading you back in to a life of fear," causing doubt and wrenching uncertainty, "but a Spirit that makes us sons, enabling us to cry 'Abba! Father!' " (Rom. 8:15). Justified by faith, they have the peace of God ruling in their hearts, flowing from a continual sense of God's pardoning mercy, as well as "the appeal made to God by a good conscience" (1 Pet. 3:21).

Some may say: "What if certain believers in Christ lose sight of the mercy of God? Suppose they no longer see the invisible God and no longer feel that quiet witness within that they are indeed recipients of Christ's atoning work. Suppose they feel utterly condemned, as if to hear again the previous sentence of death pronounced within themselves?" I answer: Let us take the supposition that a sincere believer completely loses sight of the mercy of God. At precisely that point it is difficult unambiguously to call one a believer in the full sense. For faith implies present light—the light of God shining upon the soul. Insofar as anyone loses this light, one loses touch with one's faith for that time. No doubt an earnest believer in Christ may at times lose the clear light of faith. And insofar as faith is lost, one may, for a time, fall again into a sense of condemnation. But this is not the case of those who are now "in Christ Jesus," who at this moment trust in Christ's mercy. For just as long as they believe and walk according to the Spirit, there is no condemnation either from God or from their own hearts.

2. Freedom from Present Sins

They are not condemned, secondly, for any present sins, for now transgressing the commandments of God; because insofar as they are faithful they are not now transgressing. They do not now walk after corrupted nature, but after the Spirit (Rom. 8:1–8). This is the ongoing demonstration of their "love of God," that they are "obedient to his word" (1 John 2:5). John's letters clearly testify that "a child of God does not commit sin, because the divine seed remains in him; he cannot be a sinner, because he is God's child" (1 John 3:9). The seed referred to here is loving, holy faith. As long as that seed of God remains in our hearts, we do not willfully sin. "We know that no child of God is a sinner; it is the Son of God who keeps him safe, and the evil one cannot touch him" (1 John 5:18). Anyone who is not committing sin is surely not being condemned for sin. "But if you are led by the Spirit, you are not under law" (Gal. 5:18), not under its curse or condemnation. For the law condemns none but those who break it. The law of God that commands, "You shall not steal" (Exod. 20:15), condemns no one except those who do, in fact, steal. You know the law that says, "Remember to keep the sabbath day holy" (Exod. 20:8). Does it condemn those who keep it holy? No, it condemns only those who do not keep it holy.

The fruits of the Spirit are love, joy, and peace. "There is no law dealing with such things as these" (Gal. 5:22, 23). The Apostle explains this more fully in his memorable words to Timothy: "We all know that the law is an excellent thing, provided we treat it as law" (1 Tim. 1:8). This assumes that we recognize —while making use of the law of God as it convicts us of sin and guides us—that the law is not aimed at those whose hearts are righteous. This does not mean that "the law is not made for a righteous man," as sometimes translated, but rather that the law "is not aimed at good citizens, but at the lawless and unruly, the impious and sinful, the irreligious and worldly; at parricides and matricides, murderers and fornicators, perverts, kidnappers, liars, perjurers—in fact all whose behaviour flouts the wholesome teaching which conforms with the gospel entrusted to me, the gospel which tells of the glory of God in his eternal felicity" (1 Tim. 1:9–11).

3. Inward Sin Remains, but Lacks Power

There is no condemnation for inward sin, even though it does still remain. In those who are the children of God by faith, the lower nature obviously still does remain, for believers continue to experience inwardly a struggle with the seeds of pride and vanity, of anger, inordinate passions, and evil desire—in fact, every imaginable kind of sin. Our daily experience confirms this. This is why Paul, in speaking to those whom he has just before said were "God's people at Corinth, dedicated to him in Christ Jesus" (1 Cor. 1:2) and who were called "to share in the life of his Son Jesus Christ or Lord" (1 Cor. 1:9), nonetheless turns immediately to the same persons and says: "For my part, my brothers, I could not speak to you as I should speak to people who have the Spirit. I had to deal with you on the merely natural plane, as infants in Christ"

(I Cor. 3:1). They were indeed "in Christ." They were believers in a low degree. Yet they remained "infants in Christ." Even though they had begun to be "in Christ," yet much remained in them of sin and of "the lower nature" that is "not subject to the law of God" (Rom. 8:7)!

Yet, even with these remaining encumberances, they are not condemned. They may keenly feel the weight of their lower nature in themselves. They may grow more aware daily that their "heart is the most deceitful of all things, desperately sick" (Jer. 17:9). Yet as long as they do not yield to it, and as long as they do not make room in themselves for the devil, and as long as they maintain a continual war with all sin, with pride, anger, and inordinate desire, so that the lower nature does not rule over them, they still "walk after the Spirit"; and therefore "there is no condemnation for those who are united with Christ Jesus" (Rom. 8:1). God is well pleased with their sincere, though imperfect, response. Thus they may have confidence in God, for "this is how we can make sure that he dwells within us: we know it from the Spirit he has given us" (I John 3:24).

There is no condemnation, even though believers are realistically aware that sin clings to all they do. Even though they are conscious of not fulfilling the perfect law in their thoughts, words, and works, they are not condemned. Even though they know they do not fully love the Lord their God with all their heart and mind and soul and strength, they are not condemned. Even though they may feel some pride or self-will stealing in and mixing with the best performance of their duties, they are not condemned.

Even when—in their more immediate intercourse with God in worship, when they pour out their souls in secret to God who sees all the thoughts and intentions of their hearts—they are continually plagued by wandering thoughts or awareness of the deadness and dullness of their affections, still there is no condemnation to them either from God or from their own heart. For their awareness of these many defects only gives them a deeper sense that they always have need of the sacrifice of Christ the Advocate who speaks for them in the presence of God. "This is why he is also able to save absolutely those who approach God through him; he is always living to plead on their behalf" (Heb. 7:25). These difficulties do not drive believers away from Christ in whom they have believed, but rather they drive them closer to Christ, whose compassion they feel the need of every moment. Paradoxically, the deeper sense they have of their own deficiencies, the more earnestly they feel their desire for Christ, and the more diligent they become. "Therefore, since Jesus was delivered to you as Christ and Lord, live your lives in union with him" (Col. 2:6).

4. Involuntary Failings Not Condemned

There is no condemnation for "sins of infirmity," as they are sometimes called, resulting from involuntary defects of our human finitude. Perhaps it is better instead to call them simply *"infirmities,"* or "human frailties," in order that we may not seem to lend legitimacy to sin, or to excuse it in any way by coupling it too directly with human finitude. Although "sin of infirmity" remains an ambiguous and somewhat dangerous expression, by it I mean primarily involuntary failings. One example would be saying something we believe to be true, though in fact it later proves to be false. Another example: hurting our neighbor without knowing or intending it, or even when we intended to do good. Although these are deviations from the holy, acceptable, and perfect will of God, yet they should not properly be called sins because they lack the element of being willed. Thus they do not add any guilt to the conscience of "those who are in Christ Jesus." They cause no alienation or breach between God and the faithful. They do not cloud the light of God's shining. They are in no way inconsistent with the general character of one who "walks not after the lower nature, but after the Spirit."

There is no condemnation to believers for anything conceivable that is beyond their power to prevent. This refers both to inward attitudes and outward actions, both to doing something and to leaving something undone. For example, suppose the Lord's Supper is celebrated but you do not partake of it because of sickness—an omission indeed, but one you cannot help. There is here no condemnation and no guilt, because there is no choice. Paul writes: "Provided there is an eager desire to give, God accepts what a man has; he does not ask for what he has not" (2 Cor. 8:12). . . .

Then there are so-called sins of surprise; for example, when one who is usually patient speaks or acts in a way that violates the command to love the neighbor due to some sudden or violent temptation. These cases are far more difficult to analyze. It is not easy to fix a general rule concerning misdeeds of this sort. We cannot flatly say either that persons are or are not condemned for these types of highly uncharacteristic behavior. Whenever a believer is overtaken in a fault by surprise, however, there must be some degree of guilt proportional to the degree of concurrence of the will. In proportion as a sinful desire, word, or action is more or less voluntary, so we may suppose that God is more or less displeased; and there is more or less of a burden of guilt to bear.

If so, then there may be some "sins of surprise" that rightly elicit a sense of guilt and condemnation. Admittedly, in some instances our being surprised is due to some willful and culpable neglect. Perhaps we could have been attentive to something that could have been prevented or shaken off before the temptation came. We might have been adequately forwarned that trials and dangers were at hand and yet have said in our hearts: "A little more slumber, a little more folding of the hands in rest." Suppose one later falls unaware into a trap that might easily have been avoided. Inattentiveness is hardly an excuse, for one might have foreseen and averted the danger. Falling, even by surprise, in such an instance as this is, in effect, a willful sin and, as such, must expose the sinner to condemnation, both from God and from one's own conscience.

On the other hand, there may be sudden assaults, either from the world or the god of this world, and frequently from our own distorted imaginings, which we did not, and hardly could have, foreseen. Believers who are weak in faith may be overcome by these assaults; they may become inordinately angry or think badly of others with only a very slight concurrence of the will. In such a case, God—who jealously cares for their souls—would undoubtedly show them that they have acted foolishly, in order to convince them that they had swerved away from the perfect law, from the mind which was in Christ. Consequently, they would feel grieved with a godly sorrow and lovingly ashamed before God. But they do not need to feel condemned. God does not charge them with folly, but has compassion, even "as a father has compassion on his children" (Ps. 103:12). This is why their hearts do not condemn them. For even in the midst of that sorrow and shame they can still say:

> God is indeed my deliverer.
> I am confident and unafraid;
> for the LORD is my refuge and defence
> and has shown himself my deliverer.
> And so you shall draw water with joy
> from the springs of deliverance. (Isa. 12:2)

Take the First Steps

It is fitting that we try to draw some practical inferences from all this.

1.   Away with Fears

Why are you afraid of your past? For there is now no condemnation of past sins "for those who are united with Christ Jesus" (Rom. 8:1), when the "law of the Spirit has set you free" (Rom. 8:1). O you of little faith! Even though your sins were once more in number than the sand, so what? You are now in Christ Jesus! "Who will be the accuser of God's chosen ones? It is God who pronounces acquittal; then who can condemn?" (Rom. 8:33).

All the sins you have committed from your childhood right up to the moment when you were "accepted as his sons through Jesus Christ" (Eph. 1:5) are driven away as chaff. They are gone. They are lost. They are swallowed up. They are remembered no more. You are now "born" from spirit (John 3:6). Why are you afraid? Why be troubled even about what happened before you were born? Throw away your fears! "For the spirit that God gave us is no craven spirit, but one to inspire strength, love, and self-discipline" (2 Tim. 1:7). Know your calling! Rejoice in God your Savior and give thanks to God your Father through Him.

Some will say, "But I have once again done serious

wrongs, even after receiving this redemption. I seem like a lost cause. I still feel deep remorse." It is fitting that you feel a proportional remorse after doing wrong. For it is God who has awakened this very feeling in you. But you are now invited to transcend it in trust. Hasn't the Spirit also enabled you to say, "But in my heart I know that my vindicator lives, and that he will rise last to speak in court" (Job 19:25); and "the life I now live is not my life, but the life which Christ lives in me; and my present bodily life is lived by faith in the Son of God" (Gal. 2:20)? It is that faith that cancels all that is past, and in it there is no condemnation. At whatever time you truly believe in the name of the Son of God, all your sins prior to that time vanish like the morning dew. "Christ set us free, to be free men. Stand firm, then, and refuse to be tied to the yoke of slavery again" (Gal. 5:1). Christ has once again made you free from the power of sin, as well as from its guilt and punishment. So do not become entangled again in the yoke of bondage—its twisted desires, distorted emotions, its vile words and works, the most desperate bondage this side of hell. Refuse to be caught again in bondage to slavish, tormenting fear or self-condemning guilt.

2. If Your Heart Condemns You, God Is Greater Than Your Heart

Those who are "united with Christ Jesus" manifest this union in their actions. They walk not after the corrupted nature, but after the Spirit. Shall we conclude that those who are now doing wrong have temporarily forfeited that participation in Christ? Indeed, those now sinning find themselves condemned in their own hearts. But remember: "Even if our conscience condemns us," even if our moral awareness discloses all too clearly that we are guilty, nonetheless "God is greater than our conscience and knows all" (1 John 3:20). We cannot deceive God, even if we can deceive ourselves.

So, while sinning, please do not make a show of saying: "I was justified once before, and my sins were forgiven." What happened long ago is something I cannot know and will not dispute. At this distance of time it may be next to impossible to know with any tolerable degree of certainty whether that was a true, genuine work of God, or whether you are deceiving yourself. But this I know with the utmost degree of certainty: it is the one who "does right who is righteous, as God is righteous; the man who sins is a child of the devil" (1 John 3:7–8). So insofar as you sin, your behavior is showing you to be a child of that alien father. Do not try to sin and claim righteousness. Do not flatter yourself with empty hopes! Do not say to your soul, "Be at ease," when there can be no peace. Instead cry aloud! Out of the depths, cry to God, hoping that God may hear your voice. Come again to God just as you had come before, as wretched and poor, as sinful, miserable, blind, and naked! And take care that you do not permit yourself to rest easily until his pardoning love again is revealed, until you heal your backslidings and know again that "the only thing that counts is faith active in love" (Gal. 5:6).

3. Face Yourself Candidly

There is no condemnation for any inward sin still remaining in those who "walk by the Spirit." Even though sin may seem to cling tenaciously to everything we do, we are not guilty as long as we do not give way to it. So do not be disturbed because some ungodly imaginations remain in your heart. Do not feel dejection because you still come short of the glorious image of God; or because pride, self-will, or unbelief cling to all your words and works. Do not be afraid to face candidly all these distortions of your heart. Know yourself as you are known. Desire fervently of God that you may not think more highly of yourself than you ought to think. Let your continuous prayer be:

> Show me, as my soul can bear,
> The depth of inbred sin;
> All the unbelief declare,
> The pride that lurks within.

As God hears your prayer, he will let you see your heart. Then he will show you in entirety the spirit to which you belong. Then take care that your faith does not fail you, or that your protection is not torn from you. Now you are free to see yourself quite openly even at your lowest, to be humbled in the dust, to see yourself as nothing, less than nothing, and empty. At that very moment you may still "set your troubled hearts at rest, and banish your fears" (John 14:27). Remember that you, even you, have an Advocate "with the Father, Jesus Christ, and he is just" (1 John 2:1). Hold fast to the recollection that "as the heaven stands high above the earth" (Ps. 103:11), so is God's love higher even than my sins.

God is merciful to you, a sinner! Precisely the sinner you are! God is love, and Christ has died! That means: the Father himself loves you! You are his child! God will not withhold from you anything that is for your good. Is it not good that the whole body of sin, which is now crucified in you, should be destroyed? It shall be done! You shall be cleansed "from all that can defile flesh or spirit" (2 Cor. 7:1). Is it not good that nothing should remain in your heart but the pure love of God alone? Take joy in all of this. "Love the Lord your God with all your heart, with all your soul, with all your mind, and with all your strength"; and "love your neighbour as yourself" (Mark 12:30, 31). Stand firm in the "conviction of his power to do what he had promised" (Rom. 4:21). It is your part patiently to continue in the work of faith and the labor of love, in cheerful peace, humble confidence, and with calm and accepting, but fervant, expectation, to wait until the zeal of the Lord of hosts shall perform this work in you.

4. Leap and Walk!

If those who are "in Christ" and "walk in the Spirit" are not condemned for sins of infirmity or for involuntary failings or for anything they are unable to prevent, then take care, all you who have newly born faith in God's mercy, that you do not just at this point give the devil a huge advantage. You are still unformed and weak, lacking in clear insight and deep knowledge. You are more vulnerable than words can express, more prone to error than you can imagine. For you do not yet understand faith as fully as you intend. So do not let this weakness and untested judgment, or any of its fruits which you are not yet able to avoid, shake your basic faith, your filial trust in God, or disturb your peace or joy in the Lord. The very idea that sin must be willed can itself be dangerously misapplied, so it is wiser and safer if it is applied only to the case of weakness and infirmities.

If you have stumbled, O seeker of God, do not just lie there fretting and bemoaning your weakness! Patiently pray: "Lord, I acknowledge that every moment I would be stumbling if you were not upholding me." And then get up! Leap! Walk! Go on your way! "Run with resolution the race" in which you are entered (Heb. 12:1).

My last point: Even if you find yourself for a moment to your amazement doing exactly what your soul otherwise detests, this is still not reason to feel overburdening guilt. Let us hope that your being surprised is not due to your own carelessness or willful neglect. If, while you believe, you are suddenly overtaken in a fault, then let the Lord immediately hear your cry of grief. It will then be felt by you as a healing ointment. Pour out your heart before God. Declare your trouble. Pray with all your might to God who is fully able "to sympathize with our weaknesses" (Heb. 4:15). God wants to establish, strengthen, and settle your soul and not allow you to fall again; but, meanwhile, God is not harshly disapproving of you. So why should you be afraid? You have no reason to fall into the grip of the fear that "brings with it the pains of judgment" (1 John 4:18).

Just love God who loves you. That is sufficient. The more deeply you love, the stronger you will feel. And as soon as you have learned to love God with all your heart, "if you give fortitude full play you will go on to complete a balanced character that will fall short in nothing" (James 1:4). Wait in peace for that hour when "God himself, the God of peace," will "make you holy in every part, and keep you sound in spirit, soul, and body, without fault when Our Lord Jesus Christ comes" (1 Thess. 5:23)!

Teach me to ask and seek only those things that will please thee and strengthen my soul. Give me such a measure of thy grace that I may walk the way of thy commandments, obtain thy gracious promises, and share thy eternal blessings. Pour down upon me the fullness of thy mercy. Give me more than I can either desire or deserve. O give me the increase of faith, hope, and love; and by thy assistance, keep me always from all things hurtful, and lead me to all things useful. Let thy grace go before me and follow me, that I may be continually given to all good works, and may always glorify my Father in heaven. Amen. (*WJW* XI, 265)

Thou hidden Source of calm repose,
Thou all-sufficient Love divine,
My Help and Refuge from my foes,
Secure I am, if Thou art mine;
And lo! from sin and grief and shame
I hide me, Jesus, in Thy name.

Thy mighty Name salvation is,
And keeps my happy soul above;
Comfort it brings, and pow'r, and peace,
And joy, and everlasting love;
To me, with Thy great Name, are given
Pardon and holiness and heaven.

Jesus, my All in All Thou art:
My Rest in toil, my ease in pain,
The med'cine of my broken heart,
In war my peace, in loss my gain,

My smile beneath the tyrant's frown,
In shame my glory and my crown!

In want my plentiful supply,
In weakness my almighty pow'r,
In bonds my perfect liberty,
My light in Satan's darkest hour,
In grief my joy unspeakable,
My life in death, my heav'n in hell!

(*WH* 40)

- THREE -

The Spirit of Bondage and of Adoption

The Spirit you have received is not a spirit of slavery leading you back into a life of fear, but a Spirit that makes us sons, enabling us to cry "Abba! Father!" (Rom. 8:15)

St. Paul is speaking to those who are children of God by faith: "For all who are moved by the Spirit of God are sons of God" (Rom. 8:14). The Spirit does not lead us "back into a life of fear" (Rom. 8:15); rather, "To prove that you are sons, God has sent into our hearts the Spirit of his Son, crying 'Abba! Father!' " (Gal. 4:6). The Spirit we have received "makes us sons, enabling us to cry 'Abba! Father!' " (Rom. 8:15).

The spirit of bondage and fear is entirely different from this loving Spirit of adoption. Those who are influenced only by slavish fear cannot fully be called "sons and daughters of God," even though some may rightly be called "servants" who are "not far from the kingdom of God" (Mark 12:34).

Regrettably, the bulk of humanity and even of the so-called Christian world has not come far enough to understand even servanthood, much less the promise of becoming sons and daughters of God. For the majority "leave no place for God" in all their schemes (Ps. 10:4). Few can be said truly to love God. Perhaps a few more fear God. But the greater portion of humanity has neither the fear of God before their eyes nor the love of God in their hearts.

Some of you by God's mercy now share in a better spirit. You may remember the time when you were like this, living a condemned life. But remember carefully: At the time you were enmeshed in it, wallowing daily in deplorable misdeeds, you were not even aware of it. Yet in due time you were awakened to receive the "spirit of fear." Only later could you see that you received this spirit, for this, too, was a gift of God, a stage on the way toward the Spirit of love, which later was to fill your heart after fear had vanished away.

This text encompasses three major stages, or states, of the human condition. The first state of mind, lacking both fear and love of God, is in scripture called "natural man" or one "who is unspiritual" (1 Cor. 2:14). Secondly, one who is under the spirit of bondage and fear is sometimes said to be "under the law" (but keep in mind that this expression also signifies one who is under the Jewish dispensation, who is obliged to observe all the rites and ceremonies of Levitical law). The third stage concerns those who have exchanged the spirit of fear for the Spirit of love, who are appropriately said to be living "under grace."

Since it is of utmost importance for each of us to

know which of these states we are in, I shall point out the main features of (1) the natural human condition, (2) humanity "under the law," and (3) humanity "under grace."

The Natural Human Condition

1. Asleep to the Spirit

Scripture represents the natural human condition as a state of sleep. At this early stage the voice of God simply says: "Awake, sleeper!" (Eph. 5:14). It is the inmost life of the person, the soul, that is in a deep sleep. The spiritual senses are not yet waked up and do not recognize either spiritual good or evil. The eyes of understanding are closed shut, sealed together. They see nothing in the spiritual order, only clouds and darkness, groping as if in "a valley dark as death" (Ps. 23).

Lacking any sensitivity to spiritual reality, with all the avenues of spiritual discernment shut off, those in the natural human condition remain in gross, stupid ignorance of what we most need to know. We know nothing about God as it rightly should be known. We live as complete strangers to the law of God, failing to grasp its true, inward, spiritual meaning. We have not the vaguest conception of that holiness of heart and life that flows from the Gospel, without which no one shall behold the Lord. There is not even a slight recognition of that incomparable happiness enjoyed by those whose "life lies hidden with Christ in God" (Col. 3:3).

2. Lack of Moral Awareness

For this very reason, because we are fast asleep, we are in some sense at rest. Precisely because we are blind, we feel secure, reassuring ourselves: "Tush. No harm will happen to me." The darkness that enshrouds us keeps us settled into a kind of "peace," indeed a dangerous sort of peace, that is not even aware of the hazards at hand. Even if we stood at the edge of a moral abyss, we would fear nothing, because we are sound asleep to these dangers. We do not show anxiety over a supposed threat that we do not even recognize. We do not have sufficient understanding to fear. This is why the natural condition has so little anxiety, because it remains ignorant of God's holiness. We may not be blatantly saying in our hearts, "there is no God" (Ps. 14:1) or pretending to sit "throned on the vaulted roof of earth, whose inhabitants are like grasshoppers" (Isa. 40:22). We are more likely to be found simply trying to satisfy ourselves in the way of Epicurus.

We may talk loosely of "God's mercy," while confusing the whole idea of mercy by neglecting the fact that the holy God detests sin. In this way we imagine that God's justice, wisdom, and truth are all swallowed up into a cheap idea of mercy. In the natural stage we do not experience dread of the divine rejection that is certain to come to those who plead ignorance of the divine command. We imagine that the main point of life is merely not to cause trouble. It never enters our minds that the law of God addresses the whole range of passions, the emotive life, every thought and movement of the heart. We imagine that all our obligations have in fact been met. We rationalize that Christ came to "abolish the Law and the prophets" (Matt. 5:17).

We talk as if Christ came to save people *in,* not *from,* their sins. We assume that we will be ushered effortlessly to heaven without any commitment on our part. We forget Jesus' insistence that "not a letter, not a stroke, will disappear from the Law until all that must happen has happened" (Matt. 5:18). We ignore the hard word that "not everyone who calls me 'Lord, Lord' will enter the kingdom of Heaven, but only those who do the will of my heavenly Father" (Matt. 7:21).

Meanwhile, we remain quite naive about our own tendencies to self-deception. If we talk loosely of "repenting by-and-by" we are careful not to set an exact time. We take it for granted that some time before death we will be given the opportunity to choose, if we wish, to change our way of life. It is all thought to lie simply within our power of choice. For what could possibly hinder us from changing our behavior, if we really wanted to? All one would need is the resolution to do it! So we imagine.

3. Dependence upon Imagined Rationality and Freedom

But this ignorance never so strongly glares as in those who are termed persons of learning. Suppose "the natural man" is an "educator." Such people can talk at length of their rational faculties, of the freedom of will and the absolute necessity of such freedom in order to constitute human moral agency. They read and argue and prove through demonstrations that everyone may do as they will. All can choose their inclination toward good or evil as they prefer. In this way "their unbelieving minds are so blinded by the god of this passing age, that the gospel of the glory of Christ, who is the very image of God, cannot dawn upon them and bring them light" (2 Cor. 4:4).

From the same ignorance of ourselves and God, there may sometimes arise in natural awareness a kind of joy in which we congratulate ourselves upon our own wisdom and goodness. We may seem often to possess what the world calls "joy" and may have pleasure in gratifying immediate desires, particularly if we have large possessions. If we enjoy an affluent fortune, then we may clothe ourselves like the "rich man, who dressed in purple and the finest linen, and feasted in great magnificence every day" (Luke 16:19), for whom only death could reveal his radical dependence upon the poor. As long as we are doing well for ourselves in the natural state, many will doubtless speak well of us. They will say, "Aren't they happy people!" But this may be all that our joy amounts to: dressing up, chatter, eating, drinking, and self-amusement.

Is it not surprising that in such circumstances as these, giddy with the opiates of flattery and sin, we should imagine, among other waking dreams, that we walk in great liberty? How easy we find it to persuade ourselves that we are at liberty from all vulgar errors and from all the prejudices of a narrow education, judging exactly right and keeping clear of all extremes. We say confidently to ourselves: "I am free from all the unseemly enthusiasm of weak and narrow souls; and from superstition, the disease of fools and cowards who are always righteous over much. And how good it is to be free from the bigotry that always goes along with those who do not have a free and generous way of thinking." Meanwhile, we remain altogether free of "the wisdom from above" (James 3:17) that comes from holiness, from the religion of the heart, and from the whole mind that was in Christ.

All this time we remain deeply in bondage to sin, continuing to reinforce the habits of sin, more or less, day by day. Yet we feel ourselves to be in no trouble. If asked whether we are in bondage, we would quickly say, "Of course not!" We feel no dreadful guilt. We may halfheartedly believe that Christian revelation is from God, but we content ourselves with various evasions concerning our ongoing misdeeds, saying: "Humanity is frail. We are all weak. Everyone has human weaknesses." We may even be clever enough to quote the Scripture that "the good man may fall seven times" (Prov. 24:16), and that every day! We are prone to argue that those who imagine that anyone can be better than anyone else must be either hypocrites or enthusiasts.

If at any time a troubled thought emerges on the

edges of our consciousness concerning our potential guilt before God, we stifle it as soon as possible: "Why should I fear—isn't God merciful and didn't Christ die for sinners?" In this way we remain willing servants of sin, content with the bondage of corruption, and satisfied with ourselves both inwardly and outwardly. Not only do we remain content with not conquering sin, but also with not even making any effort to conquer sin, particularly that sin that most easily besets us.

Such is the condition of natural human existence. It may admit of varying degrees. One may be a gross and scandalous offender, while another may appear to be a much more reputable and decent sinner, having the form, though not the power, of godliness. Now we ask: is it ever possible that such persons might become awakened to their moral condition? How is it conceivable that such persons could be brought to the point even of an elementary self-recognition, become aware of moral responsibility, turn their behavior around, and enter into a new stage of utter seriousness before God? If so, they may grow toward receiving what Paul called the spirit of bondage to fear.

Life Under the Law

By some awful providence it may occur that God touches the heart of such a person who lies asleep in darkness and in the shadow of death. It may happen that the word of Scripture becomes powerfully applied to some circumstance through the power of the Spirit.

1. The Rude Awakening

Through some such occurrence natural existence becomes terribly shaken out of its deep sleep, awakening abruptly into a consciousness of danger. It may occur in a moment, or it may occur by slow degrees, that the eyes of our understanding are opened. Now for the first time the veil is partly removed, and we discern the real condition we are in.

Horrid light breaks in upon the soul, a light so bright that it may seem to gleam from a bottomless pit, from the lowest abyss, as if from hell itself. At last the person begins to grasp that the loving, merciful God is also "a devouring fire" (Heb. 12:29), a just God, awesome in holiness, judging everyone absolutely fairly in terms of their deeds. This holy God enters into judgment with the ungodly for every idle word and even for the imaginations of the heart.

The awakened person now clearly perceives that the Almighty God is "too pure to look upon evil" and will not "countenance wrongdoing" (Hab. 1:13); that God is capable of avenging every wrong done in creation and of making every account straight with evildoers. Now one realizes that "it is a terrible thing to fall into the hands of the living God" (Heb. 10:31).

The inward and spiritual meaning of the law of God now begins to glare upon us. We become aware that God's "commandment has no limit" (Ps. 119:96), and there is nothing "hidden from his heat" (Ps. 19:6). We gradually become convinced that every aspect of

God's command addresses us, referring not merely to outward acts of sin, but also to what passes in the secret recesses of the soul, which no eye but God's can penetrate.

Now if we should hear the phrase, "You shall not commit murder" (Exod. 20:13), the thunder of God's command echoes: "Everyone who hates his brother is a murderer" (1 John 3:15). And echoes again: "Anyone who nurses anger against his brother must be brought to judgment" (Matt. 5:22). Now if we hear the law say, "You shall not commit adultery" (Exod. 20:14), the voice of the Lord continues ringing in our ears, that if one looks on another "with a lustful eye he has already committed adultery" in the heart (Matt. 5:28). So at every point we feel the word of God as "alive and active. It cuts more keenly than any two-edged sword, piercing as far as the place where life and spirit, joints and marrow, divide" (Heb. 4:13). This becomes all the more penetrating as we become conscious of having already neglected so great a salvation (Heb. 2:3); and of "how much more severe a penalty that man will deserve who has trampled under foot the Son of God," who only wishes to save us from our sins, or who has "profaned the blood of the covenant by which he was consecrated" as if it were a common, unsanctifying thing (Heb. 10:29).

2. Every Motive Is Laid Bare

We become more and more aware that "there is nothing in creation that can hide from him; everything lies naked and exposed to the eyes of the One with whom we have to reckon" (Heb. 4:13). We feel ourselves to be naked, stripped of all the fig leaves we had clumsily sewed together, deprived of all our petty pretenses to religion and virtue. All our flimsy excuses before God for our sins are stripped away.

We now feel ourselves to be—as if we were victims of an ancient sacrifice—split apart, cut asunder as it were from the neck downward, so that everything within us is fully exposed. Our hearts are laid bare, and we see how deeply sin has infected us. Now we know that "the heart is the most deceitful of all things, desperately sick; who can fathom it?" (Jer. 17:9). Nothing has escaped being corrupted.

It is impossible for us to express our horror at ourselves. It seems as if nothing at all good is left in us, only unrighteousness and ungodliness. Every slight movement of the self, every temper and thought appears to be only and continually evil. Now we begin not only to see, but feel within ourselves, a revulsion so deep it cannot be described. We well know that a "worthless tree" cannot produce "good fruit" (Luke 6:43). We become desperately aware, due to the depths of our sin, that we deserve to be rejected by God, to be cast into the fire that "is not quenched" (Mark 9:48). We feel that "the wage," the fair payment, "of sin," of our own willful sin, "is death" (Rom. 6:23), even a "second death, in the lake that burns" (Rev. 21:8), the final and just end to our being.

By now the pleasant dream of the natural stage is ended. We now recognize it as a delusive fantasy, a false peace, a pretended security. The joy we then felt has now vanished like a cloud. The pleasures in which we once delighted we love no more. They pall upon the taste. It is as if too much of the sweet taste made us nauseous. We are tired of their smell. The shadows of imagined happiness flee away and sink into oblivion. Stripped of everything, we wander aimlessly, seeking rest but finding none.

3.   The Anguish of the Wounded Spirit

Now that the fumes of these opiates are dispelled, we feel more directly the anguish of a wounded spirit. We find that when we permit sin to take charge of our lives, it wreaks unmeasurable miseries. We now are better able to feel the effects of our pride, anger, corrupted desires, arbitrary self-will, malice, envy, revenge, and much more. We now feel more clearly the sorrow of our hearts for the deeper joys we have lost. We feel remorse that we have harmed ourselves in these ways, inviting a curse to come upon our lives. We are aware that we have despised our own deepest interests.

The anguish we feel hinges on our acute sense of the anger of the holy God toward sin and the consequences of divine judgment. We are not in error to fear this divine justice. We see it hanging over our heads. This is why we so deeply fear death. It looms before us as a gate to destruction, an entryway to the eternal separation of our sin from God's holiness. We fear the devil as the executioner of eternal vengeance. We may even come finally to fear ourselves most of all, imagining that if we were able to kill our own bodies we would immediately plunge both body and soul into hell. These unmanageable anxieties sometimes rise to such a great height that the wretched, disquieted, guilt-laden soul may become terrified with everything.

Then we even become afraid of nothing. We fear shadows. We are afraid of a leaf shaking in the wind. Sometimes these anxieties may even border upon wild imaginings, as if we were "drunk but not with wine" (Isa. 29:9). The proper exercise of memory and understanding may become completely suspended. All the natural faculties are affected. Sometimes these anxieties may even bring us to the brink of complete despair, so that one who is anxious about the word "death" may seem to be ready to plunge into death at any moment or in desperation to say, "I would rather be choked outright; I would prefer death to all my sufferings" (Job 7:15). It is understandable that such a person cries out, like Job of old, amid the tribulation of his heart, complaining that one's "spirit may sustain him in sickness, but if the spirit is wounded, who can mend it?" (Prov. 18:14).

4. The Bondage of the Will

Now we truly desire to break loose from sin. We begin to struggle with it. But though we strive with all our might, we cannot conquer. Sin is stronger than the will. We long eagerly to escape, but remain tightly bound in prison. We make resolutions against sin, but continue to sin again. We recognize the traps into which we get ourselves, abhor them, and yet run into them repeatedly. Does the exalted power of reason help us here? Only to make us recognize our guilt and therefore increase our misery! Such is the highly esteemed "freedom of the will"—free only to do badly, we "lap up evil like water!" (Job 15:16). Free only to wander farther and farther from the living God, we "affront God's gracious Spirit" (Heb. 10:29).

The more desperately we struggle, wish, and work to free ourselves, the more do the chains seem to tighten. The chains of sin are heavy. We wrestle to "escape from the devil's snare" in which we have been "caught and held," unable freely to will (2 Tim. 2:26). Yet no matter how much we desire to be free, we remain servants of sin. We try to rebel but we cannot win. We remain in fear and bondage to sin both outwardly and inwardly. We become anxious about those outward sins to which we are particularly prone, either by inclination, custom, or outward circumstances. We then become anxious about inward sins—those twisted emotions and skewed affections. The more we worry about sin's power, the more power it seems to have. We may bite at, but cannot break, our chains.

Thus we struggle endlessly in a cycle of remorse and sin, repenting and misjudging, until finally we come to our wits' end. Wretched, helpless, and lost, we can barely groan: "Miserable creature that I am, who is there to rescue me out of this body doomed to death?" (Rom. 7:24).

We are describing one who lives "under the law,"

and, therefore, under the "spirit of bondage and fear." It is powerfully set forth by the Apostle in Romans, chapter seven, as he speaks in the person of one who, having been awakened to new life, remembers his life "under the law": "There was a time when, in the absence of law, I was fully alive" (Rom. 7:9). I had much life, wisdom, strength, and virtue, or at least I thought so. "But when the commandment came, sin sprang to life and I died." When the commandment, in its spiritual meaning, came to my heart, my inveterate tendency to sin became stirred up and inflamed, and my pretenses to virtue died away. All this occurred by the power of God. "The commandment which should have led to life proved in my experience to lead to death, because sin found its opportunity in the commandment, seduced me, and through the commandment killed me" (Rom. 7: 10, 11). The commandment came upon me unaware. It slew my hopes. It plainly showed me, even in the midst of my apparent vitality, that I was dead. "Therefore," Paul continues, "the law is in itself holy, and the commandment is holy and just and good" (Rom. 7:12). I cannot directly lay the blame on God's commandment, just because it revealed the corruption of my own heart. Rather sin "used a good thing to bring about my death, and so, through the commandment, sin became more sinful than ever" (Rom. 7:13). I acknowledge that "the law is spiritual; but I am not: I am unspiritual, the purchased slave of sin" (Rom. 7:14). I now can recognize both the spiritual nature of the law and my own carnal, sin-prone heart. I am living like a "slave of sin," totally in bondage, just like a slave horribly bought with money and now absolutely at the slave-owner's disposal. "For what I do is not what I want to do, but what I detest" (Rom. 7:15). What I hate, that I do. Such is the bondage under which I groan. Such is the tyranny of my hard master. "Though the will to do good is there, the deed is not. The good which I want to do, I fail to do; but what I do is the wrong which is against my will" (Rom. 18, 19). "I discover this principle, then: That when I want to do the right, only the wrong is within my reach. In my inmost self," according to the inward man, "I delight in" (and consent to) "the law of God" (Rom. 21, 22); "but I perceive that there is in my bodily members a different law, fighting against the law that my reason approves and making me a prisoner under the law that is in my members, the law of sin" (Rom. 23, 24).

This drags me right into my conqueror's chariot wheels, into the very thing which my soul abhors. "Miserable creature that I am, who is there to rescue me out of this body doomed to death?" (Rom. 24). Who shall deliver me from this helpless, dying life, from this bondage to sin and misery? Until such a deliverance occurs, "I myself," or rather that I—that alter ego I am now impersonating—that "I" may try to serve the law of God with the mind or "in my inmost self," my mind and conscience being on God's side; but nonetheless I "in my unspiritual nature" remain "a slave to the law of sin" (Rom. 25), always overwhelmed by a force I cannot resist.

How lively a portraiture this is of one who struggles "under the law"! We feel a burden that cannot be shaken off. We long for liberty, empowerment, and love, but remain in fear and bondage still! We await the time when God will answer our desperate cry: "Who is there to rescue me out of this body doomed to death?"—"God alone, through Jesus Christ our Lord!" (Rom. 25).

Life Under Grace

Only then is the miserable imprisonment ended, so that we are no longer "under the law, but under grace." We are now ready to describe the condition of evangelical existence which has found grace and acceptance in the presence of God, whom we now are enabled to call "Father." The grace and power of the Holy Spirit now reigns in the heart of those who have received this Spirit of adoption, "a Spirit that makes us sons" and daughters, "enabling us to cry 'Abba! Father!' " (Rom. 8:15).

1.   The Awakening to Unmerited Grace

Our eyes are opened, but in a quite different way than when we earlier had thought we were "awake." For now we are able to behold God's love and grace toward us. When we cry out to God in our desperation, God delivers us out of our distress (Ps. 91:15). Like Moses we pray: "Show me thy glory"—and at that moment we are able to hear a voice deep within us saying (just as the Lord replied to Moses): "I will make all my goodness pass before you, and I will pronounce in your hearing the Name JEHOVAH. I will be gracious to whom I will be gracious, and I will have compassion on whom I will have compassion" (Exod. 33:18, 19). And presently "the Lord came down in the cloud and took his place beside him and pronounced the Name JEHOVAH" (Exod. 34:5). At that moment the Lord "passed in front of him" and was made known to Moses (but not with physical eyes) as "compassionate and gracious, long-suffering, ever constant and true, maintaining constancy to thousands, forgiving iniquity, rebellion, and sin, and not sweeping the guilty clean away" (Exod. 34:6, 7).

Now a heavenly, healing light breaks in upon us. We are finally able to recognize how God suffers for us. "For the same God who said, 'Out of darkness let light shine,' has caused his light to shine within us" (2 Cor. 4:6). We behold the light of the glorious love of God, made known in Jesus Christ. In this we behold the divine "realities we do not see" by sense (Heb. 11:1). Now the "things beyond our seeing, things beyond our hearing, things beyond our imagining, all prepared by God for those who love him" (1 Cor. 2:10) are revealed: The love of God, most centrally, the pardoning love of God that is given to those who trust in Jesus.

Overpowered by this recognition, we cry out from the depths, "My Lord, and my God!" For we can now see that all our misdeeds have been laid on him! "In his own person he carried our sins to the gibbet, so that we might cease to live for sin" (1 Pet. 2:24). We now behold "the Lamb of God" who "takes away the sin of the world" (John 1:29). How clearly we now discern the sense in which "God was in Christ reconciling the world to himself" (2 Cor. 5:19). For Christ was "innocent of sin, and yet for our sake God made him one with the sinfulness of men, so that in him we might be made one with the goodness of God himself" (2 Cor. 5:21). Now we grasp how completely we have been reconciled to God "by the blood of the eternal covenant" (Heb. 13:20, 21).

2. Freedom from Guilt and Fear

Both the guilt and the power of sin now come to an end. Now we can say, "I have been crucified with Christ: the life I now live is not my life, but the life which Christ lives in me; and my present bodily life is lived by faith in the Son of God, who loved me and gave himself up for me" (Gal. 2:20). Now we feel the end of our remorse, sorrow of heart, and the anguish of a wounded spirit. God turns our heaviness into joy. The hands of the physician whose good purpose had elicited pain are now binding up our wounds.

We now experience an end to our imprisonment to the power of fear. For now our hearts stand firm, believing in the Lord. We have no reason any longer to fear the anger of God. For we know that it has been turned away, that God in Christ now looks upon us not as angry judge, but as loving parent. Consequently, there is no reason to fear the devil, who "would have no authority at all" if it had not been granted "from above" (John 19:11). Those who are heirs of the kingdom of heaven have no reason to fear hell. And why should we fear death if through death Christ has broken "the power of him who had death at his command" (Heb. 2:14). God has emancipated "those who, through fear of death, had all their lifetime been in servitude" (Heb. 2:15). Rather, "we know that if the earthly frame that houses us today should be demolished, we possess a building which God has provided—a house not made by human hands, eternal, and in heaven. In this present body we do indeed groan; we yearn to have our heavenly habitation put on over this one" (2 Cor. 5:1–3). "We groan indeed, we who are enclosed within this earthly frame," yet knowing that "God himself has shaped us for this very end; and as a pledge of it he has given us the Spirit" (2 Cor. 5:4, 5).

3. Power over Sin

"Where the Spirit of the Lord is, there is liberty" (2 Cor. 3:17), not only from guilt and fear, but from sin —the heaviest of all burdens and the worst of all bondages. Now we see that our labor has not been meaningless. The trap is sprung free. We are delivered.

We are now enabled not only to struggle against sin,

but to prevail; not only to fight, but to overcome. Paul states this powerfully in Romans 6: "We know that the man we once were has been crucified with Christ, for the destruction of the sinful self, so that we may no longer be slaves of sin" (Rom. 6:6). Therefore, "you must regard yourselves as dead to sin and alive to God" (Rom. 6:11). "So sin must no longer reign in your mortal body, exacting obedience to the body's desires. You must no longer put its several parts at sin's disposal, as implements for doing wrong. No: put yourselves at the disposal of God, as dead men raised to life; yield your bodies to him as implements for doing right" (Rom. 6:12:, 13). For now, having been "emancipated from sin," you have entered into "the service of righteousness, making for a holy life" (Rom. 6:18, 19).

Thus, having "peace with God through our Lord Jesus Christ," we are now enabled to "exult in the hope of the divine splendour that is to be ours." Having been given the power to overcome sin, even every twisted desire, temper, word, and work, we stand as living witnesses to the "liberty and splendour of the children of God" (Rom. 8:21). All of these various aspects of our adoption as children of God are grounded in faith. They all bear testimony with a single voice that the Spirit makes us sons and daughters, "enabling us to cry 'Abba! Father!' " (Rom. 8:15, 16).

It is this same Spirit which continues to work "in you, inspiring both the will and the deed, for his own chosen purpose" (Phil. 2:13). It is this same Spirit through whom "God's love has flooded our inmost heart" (Rom. 5:5). This same Spirit seeks to cleanse our hearts from all the inordinate loves of the world, from "all that panders to the appetites or entices the eyes, all the glamour" of worldly life (1 John 2:16). By this Spirit we are delivered from anger and pride, from all unworthy and inordinate affections. This Spirit intends to deliver us from evil words and works, from all unholiness of conversation, so that we will not harm anyone anywhere, but become constant in all good works.

4. The Three States of Humanity

There are several ways of summing this all up: The natural human condition neither fears nor loves God; under the law we learn to fear God; under grace we are enabled to love God. Natural existence has no awareness of the things of God, walking in complete darkness; under the law we grasp the painful awareness of divine judgment; under grace we behold the joyous light of divine grace. Again: The natural stage slumbers in a false peace that amounts to spiritual death; in the legal stage, one becomes wide awake to judgment and has no peace at all; evangelical life, in trusting in God, enjoys true peace—the peace of God ruling and filling our hearts. Or: Heathen existence, whether baptized or unbaptized, imagines itself to be free, but actually lives licentiously; legal existence, whether in the people of Israel or in anyone who lives essentially out of the law, struggles with the heavy burden of the law; Christian existence enjoys the glorious liberty of the children of God. Once more: Natural existence remains morally unawakened and sins willingly; under the law we are awakened, yet sin unwillingly; the child of God does not will to sin, but rather "it is the Son of God who keeps him safe, and the evil one cannot touch him" (1 John 5:18). Finally: The natural will neither fights nor conquers sin; under the law we fight mightily with sin, but do not conquer; under grace we fight and conquer and become even more than conquerors "through him who loved us" (Rom. 8:37).

A Call to Self-Examination

From this plain account of the threefold human condition—the natural, the legal, and the evangelical life—it becomes clear that it is not sufficient to divide humanity merely into those who are sincere and insincere. You may be completely sincere in any of these states, not only amid the "Spirit of adoption," but also amid the "spirit of bondage to fear" or when you have neither fear nor love of God. Doubtless there may be sincere, humanitarian pagans, just as there are sincere Jews and sincere Christians. This criterion alone does not by any means demonstrate that you are living in a state of acceptance with God.

"Examine yourselves: are you living the life of faith? Put yourselves to the test" (2 Cor. 13:5). When Paul asks for self-examination, it has little to do with whether we are sincere, but whether we are "living the life of faith." Give yourself a rigorous examination, because it is so important to you. Ask: What is the ruling principle of your life? Is it the love of God? Is it the fear of God? Or is it neither of these, but rather the love of the world, of pleasure, of gain, of ease, of reputation? If any of the latter, you have not come even as far as legal consciousness, or life "under the law," and you remain trapped in the natural stage. Is there some part of you that yearns for your heavenly Father, hoping to feel the Spirit of adoption through whom we are enabled to sigh, "Abba! Father!"? Or when you speak to God is it more like Jonah crying "out of the belly of Sheol"? Is your cry itself already overwhelmed with anguish and fear? Or is this whole discussion completely alien to you, and you cannot imagine what I mean?

At least pull off your mask! Take Christ seriously! Stand before God candidly! Look up to the heavens and at least own up to God everlasting that you have completely missed the point, and that you are hardly a servant of God, much less an adopted and beloved child! Whoever you are, do you live irresponsibly or not? If so, is it willingly or unwillingly? In either case, take seriously the grave admonition of John that one who "sins is a child of the devil" (1 John 3:8). If you willingly do wrong, you serve the purpose of the Enemy and will doubtless be judged as you deserve. If you unwillingly do wrong, you even more desperately serve the Enemy. In either case may God deliver you out of this bondage!

Do you struggle daily against all your inclinations to sin? Do you daily feel yourself to be victorious? If so I do not doubt that you are a child of God. Stand fast in this matchless liberty! Are you struggling, but not winning? Striving, but unable to get anywhere? If so, you have some way yet to go to become a fully matured believer in Christ. Follow faithfully, and in time you will know the Lord. But suppose you are not even struggling at all, only leading an easy, indolent, fashionable life? How dare you pretend to speak the name of Christ! You only make Christ's name an embarrassment among unbelievers. Awake, you who are sleeping! Call earnestly upon God, before it is too late!

One reason so many think of themselves more highly than they ought to think is because they do not discern accurately which one of these three conditions they are in. One complication is that the three states of soul may become mingled together to some degree in a single individual. Experience shows that the legal state, or state of fear, is frequently mixed with the natural. Few are so fast asleep in sin that they are not at some times drowsily awakened. But the Spirit of God does not just wait around until we are ready to be addressed. There are times when the Spirit intends to be heard and will be heard. At that moment the natural awareness will suddenly be plunged into fear, even if for a short time; and we will be keenly aware of our human inadequacies. We will feel deeply the burden of sin and earnestly desire "to escape from the coming retribution" (Matt. 3:7, 8). But this does not usually last long. Seldom do the arrows of conviction go deeply enough into our souls. We quickly learn to stifle the grace of God and return to wallowing in the mire.

Similarly, elements of evangelical life may become mixed inconspicuously with the legal. Few of those who have the spirit of bondage and fear remain completely without hope. The wise and gracious God rarely permits this: "For he knows how we were made, he knows full well that we are dust" (Ps. 103:14). God does not will that the human spirit should forever fail in his presence. For God knows that in human creation "a breath of life passed out from me, and by my own act I created living creatures" (Is. 57:16). Therefore, at those times when God sees some good emerging, he increases the dawning of light to those who sit in darkness. He causes some aspect of his own goodness to pass before them, to make clear that he hears our prayers. In this way we may come to glimpse the promise which by faith is revealed in Christ Jesus, even though it may be a great distance away, so that we are encouraged to "run with resolution the race for which we are entered" (Heb. 12:1).

We may also deceive ourselves by not considering how far we may improve and yet remain in a natural or legal state. We may be of a compassionate and benevolent temper and be affable, courteous, generous, friendly. We may have some degree of meekness, patience, temperance, and many other moral virtues. We may feel many motivations to shake off vice entirely and to attain higher degrees of virtue, abstaining from much evil—perhaps from all that is grossly contrary to justice, mercy, or truth. We may do much good, may feed the hungry, clothe the naked, relieve the widow and fatherless. We may attend public worship, pray in private, read many books of devotion. Yet amid all of this we still have not moved beyond the natural stage if we know neither ourselves nor God. We could do all of these things and never even approach the sphere of legal consciousness, with its spirit of anxiety over repentance, much less the sphere of evangelical existence, with its spirit of love and trust in the Gospel.

But suppose there were added to all this a deep conviction of sin, with a profound awareness of God's holiness in the presence of sin. Add to that an earnest desire to cast off every sin and to enter completely into the life of righteousness, eliciting a keen hunger for God that frequently rejoices in hope, with touches of love often glancing upon the soul. Still, all this evidence does not conclusively show that one is yet under grace and truly living the Christian faith. What is missing? The Spirit of adoption that dwells in our hearts, allowing us continually to cry, "Abba, Father!"

Beware, then, you who are called in the name of Christ, that you do not fall short of the mark of your high calling. Beware that you do not rest too easily in the natural human condition, along with many who are thought to be "decent Christians." Beware that you do not become locked in the legal state, where those who seek human esteem are so often content to live and die.

No, God has prepared better things for you. Follow faithfully until they are yours. You are not called to fear and tremble like the demonic powers, but to rejoice and love like the angels of God. "Love the Lord your God with all your heart, with all your soul, with all your mind, and with all your strength" (Mark 12:30). "Be joyful always; pray continually; give thanks whatever happens" (1 Thess. 5:16). Do the will of God "on earth as in heaven" (Matt. 6:10). "Then you will be able to discern the will of God, and to know what is good, acceptable, and perfect" (Rom. 12:2). "Offer your very selves to him: a living sacrifice, dedicated and fit for his acceptance" (Rom. 12:1)! "Only let our conduct be consistent with the level we have already reached" (Phil. 3:16). "Forgetting what is behind," let us reach out "for that which lies ahead" (Phil. 3:13), until "the God of peace" shall "make you perfect in all goodness so that you may do his will; and may he make of us what he would have us be through Jesus Christ, to whom be glory for ever and ever! Amen." (Heb. 13:21).

I am ashamed when I think how long I have lived a stranger,
yea, an enemy to thee, taking upon me to dispose of myself,
and to please myself in the main course of my life. But now
I unfeignedly desire to return unto thee, and renouncing all
interest and ownership over myself, give myself up entirely
to thee. I would be thine, and only thine for ever. Amen.
(*WJW* XI, 226)

Christ, whose glory fills the skies,
Christ, the true, the only Light,
Sun of righteousness, arise,
Triumph o'er the shades of night;
Day-Spring from on high, be near;
Day-Star, in my heart appear.

Dark and cheerless is the morn
Unaccompanied by Thee.
Joyless is the day's return
Till Thy mercy's beams I see;
Till they inward light impart,
Glad my eyes and warm my heart.

Visit, then, this soul of mine;
Pierce the gloom of sin and grief.
Fill me, Radiancy Divine;
Scatter all my unbelief.
More and more thyself display,
Shining to the perfect day.

(*WH* 152)

- FOUR -

The Marks of the New Birth

You ought not to be astonished, then, when I tell you that you must be born over again. The wind blows where it wills; you hear the sound of it, but you do not know where it comes from, or where it is going. So with everyone who is born from spirit. (John 3:4–8)

Every one who is "born from spirit," born anew, is born from God. But what does that mean—to be born again, born of God, born from spirit? What is implied in becoming a son or daughter of God or in having the Spirit of adoption (Rom. 8:15)?

We know that these gifts of God's mercy are often associated with baptism (which is in some sense even suggested by the fifth verse of our text, where Jesus said to Nicodemus that "no one can enter the kingdom of God without being born from water and spirit"). Our present purpose is to ask more specifically what gifts are received in the new birth. What marks distinguish it?

Some may argue that it is hardly necessary to provide an elaborate definition of the new birth, inasmuch as the Scripture itself does not. But the question is of deepest concern to everyone who takes seriously Jesus' remark that unless one "has been born over again," born of the spirit, one "cannot see the kingdom of God" (John 3:3). I propose to set forth the marks of the new birth in the plainest way, just as I find them laid down in Scripture.

Faith

The first mark of the new birth is the foundation of all the rest: faith. Paul wrote: "For through faith you are all sons of God in union with Christ Jesus" (Gal. 3:26).

1. To Become Children of God

John's Gospel states the point with exceptional care: "But to all who did receive him, to those who have yielded him their allegiance, he gave the right," the power, the privilege, "to become children of God" (John 1:12). So when they believed, it was not as if they were "born of human stock," as if to be explainable through natural generation. Nor were they born in a way analogous to "the fleshly desire of a human father," in a way that would not require any inward change. Rather, in faith, they were becoming "the offspring of God himself" (John 1:13). Later John's Epistle made the connection unmistakably clear: "Everyone who believes that Jesus is the Christ is a child of God" (1 John 5:1).

The faith assumed here by the Apostles is not a merely speculative idea, nor is it bare assent to the proposition that "Jesus is the Christ" or to the various propositions contained in our creed, nor to propositions contained in the Old and New Testaments. It is not merely an intellectual assent to any or all of these affirmations so as to consent abstractly to their credibility. For remember that even "the devils have faith like that, and it makes them tremble" (James 2:19). This would be tantamount to saying, unthinkably, that the devils also are born again, since it can be argued that the trembling demons assented not only to the idea that Jesus is the Christ, but also to the notion that all divinely inspired scriptures are true. The demons heard Jesus speak and also knew that he bore faithful witness as they beheld the testimony he gave of himself and the Father and saw the mighty works he did. They could not help assenting that he had come from God, yet despite this assent, they are still consigned "to the dark pits of hell, where they are reserved for judgment" (2 Pet. 2:4). So vital faith cannot be reduced simply to an assent to divine truth based upon divine testimony or miracle.

It is a "dead faith" that works only by assent. True, living, Christian faith—which if you have you are "born of God"—is far more than assent. Indeed, it does involve an act of understanding, but genuine faith is a disposition that God works in our hearts. The Anglican "Homily on Salvation" clearly affirms that the believer has "a sure trust and confidence in God, that, through the merits of Christ, his sins are forgiven, and he reconciled to the favour of God." This implies that you must first renounce self-will in order to be "found in Christ," totally rejecting all "confidence in the flesh" in order to be accepted through Christ. Without any merit of your own, having no trust in your own works or righteousness of any kind, you finally come to God as a lost, miserable, broken, self-condemned, undone, helpless sinner whose mouth is utterly stopped, and who is altogether "guilty before God." This deep feeling of remorse is what some who only understand it partially call "despair." For faith moves through this sense of sin toward a full conviction, so deep that words cannot express it, that from Christ alone comes our salvation. An earnest desire for that salvation must precede a living faith, a trust in Christ who "for us paid our ransom by His death, and fulfilled the law in his life." This living faith by which you are born from God is not only a formal belief in all the articles of our faith, but also "a true confidence of the mercy of God through our Lord Jesus Christ" ("Homily on Salvation").

2. To Break the Power of Inward and Outward Sin

An immediate and constant fruit of this faith, through which we are born of God, is power over sin. This fruit cannot be separated in any way from its root, faith, not even for an hour. Power over sin is seen at two levels: external and internal. In the outer sphere, it enables power over every evil word and work. Wherever the sacrificial action of Christ is present, it seeks to cleanse our conscience from the deadness of our former ways. In the inward sphere, power over sin purifies the heart from every unholy desire and temper.

In the sixth chapter of Romans, St. Paul has described power over sin as a fruit of faith: "Shall we persist in sin, so that there may be all the more grace? No, no! We died to sin; how can we live in it any longer?" (Rom. 6:1, 2). "We know that the man we once were has been crucified with Christ, for the destruction of the sinful self, so that we may no longer be the slaves of sin, since a dead man is no longer answerable for his sin" (Rom. 6:6). "In the same way you must regard yourselves as dead to sin and alive to God, in union with Christ Jesus. So sin must no longer reign in your mortal body, exacting obedience to the body's desires" (Rom. 6:11–12). "No: put yourselves at the disposal of God, as dead men raised to life" (Rom. 6:13). "For sin shall no longer be your master" (Rom. 6:14). "God be thanked, you, who once were slaves of sin" are now "emancipated" (Rom. 6:17–18)! The plain meaning of "God be thanked" is that although you were in the past servants of sin, now, being free from sin, you are free to become servants of righteousness.

The same invaluable privilege of the children of God, power over sin, is just as strongly asserted in John's writings, particularly with regard to actions—namely, in power over outward sin as well as inward. John writes as one astonished at the depth of the riches of the goodness of God: "How great is the love that the Father has shown to us! We were called God's children, and such we are" (1 John 3:1). Here and now, dear friends, we are God's children; what we shall be has not yet been disclosed, but we know that when it is disclosed we shall be like him, because we shall see him as he is" (1 John 3:2).

John immediately adds: "A child of God does not commit sin, because the divine seed remains in him; he cannot be a sinner, because he is God's child" (1 John 3:9). Some will at this point interject: "True: a child of God does not commit sin habitually." Habitually? Where does that come from? I do not read it there. It does not seem to be in the book! God states it more plainly: "A child of God does not commit sin." Who are you to add "habitually"? By what authority do you improve on the oracles of God? "I give this warning to everyone who is listening to the words of prophecy in this book: should anyone add to them, God will add to him the plagues described in this book" (Rev. 22:18). This is especially so when the comment you add tends to swallow up the meaning of the text itself, so that by this artful method of deceiving, the full promise of the text is lost. By human deceitfulness the power of the Scripture tends to be nullified. So take care not to "take away from the words in this book," taking away the larger meaning and spirit from them and leaving only a dead letter, lest God take away your "share in the tree of life and the Holy City, described in this book" (Rev. 22:19)!

It is better that we permit the Apostle to interpret his own words in relation to the whole tenor of his discourse: "Christ appeared, as you know, to do away with sins, and there is no sin in him." What inference does he draw from this? "No man therefore who dwells in him is a sinner; the sinner has not seen him and does not know him" (1 John 3:5, 6). In order to clarify this important teaching he states this caution explicitly: "My children, do not be misled" (1 John 3:7). John anticipated that many would try to persuade others that they could commit sin and still remain children of God. So he counters: "It is the man who does right who is righteous, as God is righteous; the man who sins is a child of the devil, for the devil has been a sinner from the first" (1 John 3:7, 8). "A child of God does not commit sin, because the divine seed remains in him; he cannot be a sinner, because he is God's child. That is the distinction between the children of God and the children of the devil: no one who does not do right is God's child" (1 John 3:9, 10). By this plain mark (sinning or not sinning), they can be distinguished. John makes the same point later in his letter: "We know that no child of God is a sinner; it is the Son of God who keeps him safe, and the evil one cannot touch him" (1 John 5:18).

3. The Peace That Faith Enjoys

Another fruit of this living faith is peace. "Therefore, now that we have been justified through faith," our sins having been crossed out, "let us continue at peace with God through our Lord Jesus Christ" (Rom. 5:1). On the night before his death, our Lord himself solemnly bequeathed this peace to all his followers: "Peace is my parting gift to you"—you who believe in God and who believe also in me—"my own peace, such as the world cannot give. Set your troubled hearts at rest, and banish your fears" (John 14:27). "I have told you all this so that in me you may find peace" (John 16:33). But what is that "peace of God, which is beyond our utmost understanding" (Phil. 4:7)? It is the serenity of soul that it has not entered into the heart of a "natural man" to conceive, and that is not possible for even the spiritual one to express.

It is a peace that all the powers of earth and hell are unable to take away. Waves and storms may beat upon it; but they cannot destroy it, because it is founded upon solid rock. It keeps watch over the hearts and minds of the children of God at all times and in all places. Whether they are in ease or in pain, in sickness or in health, in abundance or in want, they are happy in God. In every state they have learned to be content and even to give thanks to God through Christ Jesus. They are inwardly assured that whatever happens, in faith it is seen as permitted by God for their good. In all the hazards of life their hearts are anchored in trust in God.

Hope

A second scriptural mark of those who are born of God is hope. Thus Peter, speaking to all the children of God who were then scattered abroad, said, "Praise be to the God and Father of our Lord Jesus Christ, who in his great mercy gave us new birth into a living hope by the resurrection of Jesus Christ from the dead" (1 Pet. 1:3).

It is a living hope, for there can also be a dead hope, just as there can be a dead faith. A morose hope is not from God, but from the Enemy of God and humanity. Deadly hope is known by its deadliest fruit: pride. It is the parent of countless harmful words and deeds.

On the other hand, everyone who has this living hope is called to mirror God's holiness. "The One who called you is holy; like him, be holy in all your behaviour, because Scripture says, 'You shall be holy, for I am holy'" (1 Pet. 1:15). "Here and now, dear friends, we are God's children; what we shall be has not yet been disclosed, but we know that when it is disclosed we shall be like him because we shall see him as he is. Everyone who has this hope before him purifies himself, as Christ is pure" (1 John 3:2, 3).

This hope is described in the Epistle to the Hebrews as the "full assurance of faith" (Heb. 10:22), a faith in which "your hope is finally realized" (Heb. 6:11). These are the best expressions our language could afford, but they are far weaker in English than the original Greek text, which implies the testimony of our own spirit or conscience, fully assuring us that "our conduct has been governed by a devout and godly sincerity" (2 Cor. 1:12), and even more, the full assurance of the Spirit of God that "joins with our spirit in testifying that we are God's children; and if children, then heirs. We are God's heirs and Christ's fellow-heirs" (Rom. 8:16, 17). . . .

Now we are better able to grasp what Jesus meant when he said that the sorrowful are blessed, for "they shall find consolation" (Matt. 5:4). For it is now possible to believe even, and precisely, amid sorrow. Although some sorrow may precede the witness of God's Spirit with our spirit (indeed it must to some degree be felt as sorrow while we groan under fear and a sense of the judgment of God against us), yet as soon as we feel this witness within ourselves, our "grief will be turned to joy" (John 16:21). "A woman in labour is in pain because her time has come; but when the child is born she forgets the anguish in her joy that a man has been born into the world" (John 16:21). Whatever the pain, the anguish is soon forgotten in the joy of new birth.

It may be that some of you are now experiencing depression because you feel like "strangers to the community of Israel, outside God's covenants and the promise that goes with them" (Eph. 2:12). You are painfully aware that you do not have this Spirit. You may feel as though your world is "without hope and without God" (Eph. 2:12). "So it is with you: for the moment you are sad at heart," but when the Comforter comes, "then you will be joyful, and no one shall rob you of your joy" (John 16:22). You will "exult in God through our Lord Jesus, through whom we have now been granted reconciliation" (Rom. 5: 11). Through Christ "we have been allowed to enter the sphere of God's grace," this state of grace, of favor, or reconciliation with God "where we now stand. Let us exult in the hope of the divine splendour that is to be ours" (Rom. 5:2)! Let the Apostle Peter speak to you of God who in his great mercy has given us "new birth into a living hope by the resurrection of Jesus Christ from the dead! The inheritance to which we are born is one that nothing can destroy or spoil or wither. It is kept for you in heaven, and you, because you put your faith in God, are under the protection of his power until salvation comes—the salvation which is even now in readiness and will be revealed at the end of time. This is cause for great joy, even though now you smart for a little while, if need be, under trials of many kinds" (1 Pet. 1:3–6). "These trials come so that your faith may prove itself worthy of all praise, glory, and honour when Jesus Christ is revealed. You have not seen him, yet you love him; and trusting in him now without seeing him, you are transported with a joy too great for words" (1 Pet. 1:7–8).

Too great for words indeed! It is beyond human language to describe this joy in the Holy Spirit. It is that "hidden manna" that is "known to none but him that receives it" (Rev. 2:17). Although there is much about it we do not know, this much we do: that it not only remains, but overflows, in the depth of affliction. Are the consolations of God small with his children when all earthly comforts fail (Job 15:11)? Not so. It is precisely when sufferings most abound that the consolation of God's Spirit abounds.

This is why the sons and daughters of God are able in a sense to "laugh at violence" when it comes (Job 5:22)—to laugh at economic hardship, pain, hell, and the grave. For they are already acquainted with the

One who finally "holds the keys of Death and Death's domain" (Rev. 1:18). All these alien powers will in due time be bound and thrown "into the abyss" (Rev. 20:3). Even now we can hear the "loud voice proclaiming from the throne: 'Now at last God has his dwelling among men! He will dwell among them and they shall be his people, and God himself will be with them. He will wipe every tear from their eyes; there shall be an end to death, and to mourning and crying and pain; for the old order has passed away!' " (Rev. 21:3, 4).

Love

A third scriptural mark of those who are born of God—the greatest of all—is love. We speak of nothing less than "God's love," which has "flooded our inmost heart through the Holy Spirit he has given us" (Rom. 5:5). "To prove that you are sons, God has sent into our hearts the Spirit of his Son, crying 'Abba! Father!' " (Gal. 4:6).

By this Spirit, continually looking up to God as their reconciling and loving Father, the faithful pray to him for daily bread and for everything needful for their souls and bodies. They continually pour out their hearts before God, knowing that "if we make our requests which accord with his will he listens to us" (1 John 5:14). Their delight is in God, the joy of their hearts, their "shield" (Ps. 33:20), and their rich reward (Luke 6:23). The desire of their souls is turned toward God. It is their "meat and drink" to do God's will. They are "satisfied as with a rich and sumptuous feast and wake the echoes with thy praise" (Ps. 63:5).

It is in this sense, also, that "he who loves God must also love his brother. Everyone who believes that Jesus is the Christ is a child of God, and to love the parent means to love his child" (1 John 4:21–5:1). God's grace dwells "with all who love our Lord Jesus Christ" (Eph. 6:24), who rejoice in God as Savior, and who are "linked with Christ" (1 Cor. 6:17) as if at "one with him" (1 Cor. 6:17). It is as if a lover were always turned toward the beloved. Just so are believers turned toward Christ, who is beheld as altogether lovely, "a paragon among ten thousand" (Song of Songs 5:10). The believer knows and feels what this means: "My beloved is mine and I am his" (Song of Songs 2:16). "You surpass all mankind in beauty, your lips are moulded in grace, so you are blessed by God for ever" (Ps. 45:2).

The necessary fruit of this love of God is the love of our neighbor. This includes every person God has created. It includes our enemies, and those who treat us spitefully (Luke 6:28). It is a love in which we love everyone as we would wish to be loved, and as we love ourselves.

Our Lord has expressed this even more strongly, teaching us to love one another as God has loved us (1 John 4:7–12). Accordingly, the commandment written in the hearts of all those that love God is no less than this: "Love one another, as I have loved you"

(John 15:12). "It is by this that we know what love is: That Christ laid down his life for us. And we in our turn are bound," as the Apostle rightly infers, "to lay down our lives" for our brothers and sisters. If we feel ourselves ready to do this, then we truly love our neighbor. Only then have we "crossed over from death to life; this we know, because we love our brothers" (1 John 3:14). "Here is the proof that we dwell in him and he dwells in us: he has imparted his Spirit to us" (1 John 4:13). For "love is from God. Everyone who loves is a child of God and knows God" (1 John 4:7).

Some may wrongly infer from the Apostle that the love of God is not an affection of the soul, but merely an outward service; and the love of the neighbor is not a disposition of the heart, but barely a course of outward works. It would be a wild interpretation of the Apostle's words to view love only externally as an activity. The plain, indisputable meaning of 1 John 5:3 is that this is the sign or demonstration of the love of God and of our keeping the first and great commandment—that we keep all the rest of God's commandments. Having the true love of God flood our hearts will constrain us to keep God's commandments. Those who love God with all their hearts will serve God with all their strength.

Another fruit of the love of God (so intimately related to it that it is difficult to distinguish from it) is universal obedience to the God whom we love and conformity to his will. This implies obeying all the commands of God, internal and external. It is an obedience both of heart and life. It penetrates into every temper and every moment of meeting others. One of the characteristics most obviously implied is being "eager to do good" (Titus 2:14), to be hungry and thirsty to do good in every possible way to every person met. "As for me, I will gladly spend what I have for you—yes, and spend myself to the limit" (2 Cor. 12:15). For love does not look for recompense within this world, but for the resurrection of the just.

Who Is Born Again?

These three marks of the new birth—faith, hope, and love—are plainly laid out in Scripture. In this way God himself answers that weighty question: What does it mean to be born again of God? It means to be born of the Spirit and, thereby, to become empowered as a son or daughter of God in the presence of God.

To summarize: To be born again is above all to believe in God; to have faith in God through Christ, so as not to turn again to our lower nature; and to enjoy at all times and in all places that "peace of God, which is beyond our utmost understanding" (Phil 4: 7). Second, it is to have hope in God through his beloved Son so as to have within ourselves the testimony of a good conscience, accompanied by the Spirit of God joining "with our spirit in testifying that we are God's children" (Rom. 8:16). Out of this springs an everlasting joy in Christ "through whom we have now been granted reconciliation" (Rom. 5:11). Finally, it is to love God as God has loved you. It is to love God more than you ever loved any creature. It is to love others, every other person, as you love yourself. It is to love from the heart, but proceeding outwardly to all your actions and conversations, making your whole life a labor of love, lived out in continuing responsiveness to the claim of God. You are called to "be compassionate as your Father is compassionate" (Luke 6: 36). "Be holy in all your behaviour, because Scripture says, 'You shall be holy, for I am holy' " (1 Pet. 1:16). "There must be no limit to your goodness, as your heavenly Father's goodness knows no bounds" (Matt. 5:48).

If "what we have been told" is from God (Heb. 2:1), then you can be assured that this means that you are children of God: "This is how we may know that we belong to the realm of truth, and convince ourselves in his sight that even if our conscience condemns us, God is greater than our conscience" (1 John 3:19, 20)! If you have heard these words, you can then inquire of your feelings and know truthfully at this moment, answering to God alone rather than to human investigation, whether you are a child of God. The question must not be evaded by asking whether you were once baptized, but where you stand now.

Is the Spirit of adoption now in your heart? Let the question be addressed only to your own heart. I am not asking when you were baptized, but whether the

Holy Spirit is now alive in your heart. Paul wrote: "Circumcision has value, provided you keep the law; but if you break the law, then your circumcision is as if it had never been" (Rom. 2:25). The deeper question is: Does the Spirit of Christ and of glory now rest upon you?

It does not follow that, because you were once baptized, you are now a child of God in the fully matured sense. Do we have to look far to see baptized gluttons, hard drinkers, and liars, baptized troublemakers and lechers, baptized thieves and extortionists? Are you telling me that these are all now children of God? Jesus spoke sharply of these works when he said of such persons: "Your father is the devil and you choose to carry out your father's desires" (John 8:44). He denounced similarly those who thought they could rely upon their circumcision: "You viper's brood! How can your words be good when you yourselves are evil?" (Matt. 12:34).

Unless you are born again, how are you going to change, you who are now "dead in your sins and wickedness" (Eph. 2:1)? You are without hope, stamped for despair, consigned to darkness, if there is no possibility of rebirth. Yet beware of an excessive zeal that would say too quickly, "Yes, destroy the sinners, the Amalekites! Let these Gibeonites be destroyed! That is exactly what they deserve" (1 Sam. 15:17-20; 2 Sam. 21:1-9). For if God's justice alone were at work, we would all deserve that same sad judgment. I would. You would. It is only because of God's free mercy, wholly undeserved by us, that we are not now lost in darkness. If you boast, "But we were once baptized!" then we will hope that you currently show evidence of your baptism. Don't you know that "God sees through you; for what sets itself up to be admired by men is detestable in the sight of God" (Luke 16:15). Step right up, you saints of the world who enjoy the honor of baptism. Let us see which one of you is prepared to cast the first stone at the harlots, adulterers, murderers, and the wretched of the earth! It is better that you learn what John meant when he said, "Everyone who hates his brother is a murderer" (1 John 3:15), or Jesus when he said, "If a man looks on a woman with a lustful eye, he has already committed adultery with her in his heart" (Matt. 5:28). If you have become a "false, unfaithful creature," then learn how your own love of the world has become "enmity to God" (James 4:4).

"Jesus answered, 'In truth, in very truth I tell you, unless a man has been born over again he cannot see the kingdom of God'" (John 3:3). To appeal only to our baptism may be like "a splintered cane that will run into a man's hand and pierce it if he leans on it" (Isa. 36:6). Even if you were at one time made heirs of the kingdom in baptism, you must claim that baptims for your own. You must be born again.

If the heart of the matter is clear, then let us not quibble further with words. You have heard about the evidences that distinguish the children of God: faith, hope, and love. If you do not yet have them, whether baptized or unbaptized, your soul stands in need of them and without them is lost. If you have been made a child of God by baptism but have subsequently fallen away, then you may once again receive "the right to become children of God" (John 1:12); and once again receive what has been lost, namely, that Spirit of adoption that enables us to cry, "Abba! Father!" (Rom. 8:15). Amen!

Lord Jesus! May all who are preparing their hearts to seek your presence at this moment receive again that Spirit of adoption. May they cry out now to you: "Abba! Father!" Let each one once again have power to believe in your mercy so as to become a child of God. May each one know and feel that "in Christ our release is secured and our sins are forgiven through the shedding of his blood" (Eph. 1:7), looking toward your promise that those born of God are victorious over sin (1 John 3:9). Let each one now be given a "new birth into a living hope" (1 Pet. 1:3), remembering that "Everyone who has this hope before him purifies himself, as Christ is pure" (1 John 3:3). Let the Spirit of love and glory rest upon each one of your sons and daughters, that we may "cleanse ourselves from all that can defile flesh or spirit and in the fear of God complete our consecration" (2 Cor. 7:1).

Father, accept my imperfect repentance, be compassionate toward my infirmities, purify my uncleanness, strengthen my weakness, fix my unstableness, and let thy good Spirit watch over me forever, and thy love ever rule in my heart, through the merits and sufferings and love of thy Son, in whom thou art always well pleased. Amen. (*WJW* XI, 231-232)

Come, O Thou Traveler unknown,
Whom still I hold, but cannot see!
My company before is gone,
And I am left alone with thee;
With Thee all night I mean to stay,
And wrestle till the break of day.

I need not tell Thee who I am;
My misery and sin declare.
Thyself hast called me by my name;
Look on Thy hands, and read it there.
But who, I ask Thee, who art Thou?
Tell me Thy name, and tell me now.

Yield to me now; for I am weak,
But confident in self-despair.
Speak to my heart, in blessings speak;
Be conquered by my instant prayer.
Speak, or Thou never hence shalt move,
And tell me if Thy name is Love.

'Tis Love! 'tis Love! Thou diedst for me!
I hear Thy whisper in my heart;
The morning breaks, the shadows flee;
Pure, universal Love Thou art.
To me, to all, Thy mercies move;
Thy nature and Thy name is Love.

The Sun of Righteousness on me
Hath risen with healing in His wings.
Withered my nature's strength, from Thee
My soul its life and succour brings;
My help is all laid up above.
Thy nature and Thy name is Love.

(WH 28)

FIVE

On Working Out Our Own Salvation

You must work out your own salvation in fear and trembling; for it is God who works in you, inspiring both the will and the deed, for his own chosen purpose. (Phil. 2:12–13)

Some great truths, such as the being and attributes of God and the difference between moral good and evil, were in some measure known to the ancient world. The traces of them are to be found in all nations. In some sense it may be said of every human being that:

> God has told you what is good;
> and what is it that the Lord asks of you?
> Only to act justly, to love loyalty.
> to walk wisely before your God. (Mic. 6:8)

With this truth God has in some sense enlightened everyone in the world (John 1:9). Even those who "have no law"—no written law—"are their own law," for they "display the effect of the law"—the substance of it, though not the letter—for it is "inscribed on their hearts" by the same hand which wrote the commandments on tables of stone. "Their conscience is called as a witness" (Rom. 2:15) as to whether they act suitably or not.

The best of ancient (and even modern!) pagan wisdom remained totally ignorant, however, of the most important Christian teachings. These are summarized under two great divisions: justification and sanctification. I am speaking first of those truths that were revealed through the Son of God, who gave himself as a "remedy for the defilement of our sins, not our sins only but the sins of all the world" (1 John 2:2); and secondly of those relating to the Spirit of God, renewing us in that image of God in which we were created.

After all the pains which ingenious and learned thinkers have taken to find some resemblance of these truths in the immense rubbish of secular authors, the resemblance is so exceedingly faint that it cannot be discerned except by a very lively imagination. Even this resemblance, faint as it appears, is only to be found in the writings of a very few; and those were the most learned sages of their generations. Meanwhile, the multitudes that surrounded them were made little better by the achievements of these philosophers, since they remained as totally ignorant of these capital truths as were the beasts that perish.

These truths were never known to the masses or the majority of persons in any nation until they were brought to light by the Christian Gospel. Even though a spark of knowledge glimmered here and there, the whole earth remained covered with darkness until the Sun of righteousness rose up and scattered the shades of night. Since this "morning sun from heaven" has risen upon us, a great light shines out toward those who, until that time, had remained "in darkness, under the cloud of death" (Luke 1:78, 79).

Since then thousands in every age have come to know that "God loved the world so much that he gave his only Son, that everyone who has faith in him may not die but have eternal life" (John 3:16). Entrusted with the Scripture, this community has come to know how God also gives us the Holy Spirit who works in us "inspiring both the will and the deed, for his own chosen purpose" (Phil. 2:13).

How remarkable are these words of the Apostle that immediately precede our main text: "Let your bearing toward one another arise out of your life in Christ Jesus. For the divine nature"—the unfathomable essence, the incommunicable nature of God from eternity—"was his from the first; yet he did not think to snatch at equality with God" (Phil. 2:5–7). The precise meaning of this phrase is that Christ did not count it as an act of robbery or an invasion of another's prerogative, but his own unquestionable right, to be equal with God. The form of God implies both the fullness and the incomparable majesty of the Godhead. Two words are used to counterpoint this majesty: emptying and humbling. He emptied himself of that divine fullness, concealed his fullness from the eyes of rational intelligence, "made himself nothing, assuming the nature of a slave," by that very act of emptying himself. "Bearing the human likeness"—a real human being, like any other human being—"revealed in human shape"—a common individual, without any peculiar beauty or excellency—"he humbled himself" to a still greater degree and became obedient to God, though equal with him, "and in obedience accepted even death—death on a cross" (Phil. 2:7, 8) —an unparalleled example of humble obedience!

Having proclaimed Christ's pattern of obedience, the Apostle then calls his hearers to make complete the salvation that Christ has purchased for them: "Work out your own salvation in fear and trembling; for it is God who works in you, inspiring both the will and the deed, for his own chosen purpose" (Phil. 2:12, 13).

We will develop three particular themes of this wide-ranging text: First, the fundamental premise to be remembered is that "it is God who works in you, inspiring both the will and the deed, for his own chosen purpose." Second, we are then called to make our own response to God's working: "You must work out your own salvation in fear and trembling." Finally, we will deal with the dynamic connection between God's work and our work, the "therefore"; for "God works in you," therefore, "you must work" (Phil. 2:12, 13).

God Works in Us

Paul first reminds us that "it is God who works in you, inspiring both the will and the deed, for his own chosen purpose" (Phil. 2:13). The meaning of these words is made more plain by changing their order: "It is God who for his own chosen purpose works in you, inspiring both the will and the deed."

This quickly removes any fantasy that we might merit salvation. Otherwise, we might find some room for boasting, as if it were our own accomplishment, based on some goodness in us, or some good act done by us, that first motivated God to act on our behalf. But the Apostle's phrase undercuts all such vain conceits, showing that God's motive to work lies wholly within himself, in his own grace and mercy, without our meriting it.

"Willing and doing" may be interpreted in two ways, each of which contains some truth: At one level "willing" seems to refer to the whole of inward religion, while "doing" seems to imply outward religion. Understood in this way, the sentence implies that God is working in us to nurture both inward and outward holiness.

Yet a fuller interpretation is possible, if we look at the original Greek word for will, which implies the whole sphere of human desire and every emotive inclination, extending to our temperaments, words, and actions. Thus the notion of will itself already is dealing with both the inward and outward aspects of holy living. And the word we translate "to do" clearly implies more than our doing, for it refers at the same time to all that power from on high, all that divine energy that works in us to elicit every right disposition and then equips us for every good word and work.

A deep, lasting conviction of this will guard us from

falling into boastful pride. For if we are thoroughly aware that we possess nothing that we have not received, how can we boast that we have earned it? If we know and feel that the very first motion of good is from above—as well as the power which directs it every step along the way to its conclusion—and if it is God who not only awakens every good desire, but who accompanies and follows each one, then it evidently follows that anyone who boasts must "boast of the Lord" (1 Cor. 1:31).

Working Out Our Own Salvation

1. Through Preceding, Convicting, Justifying, and Sanctifying Grace

If God works in you, then you are called to work out your own salvation. "Work out" implies in the original word "doing a thing thoroughly." It must be your own. You yourselves must do this, or it will be left forever undone.

God's design for salvation begins with what is usually, and very properly, called (1) preceding grace. This has often been called prevenient grace, the grace that comes before our willing. It includes the first wish to please God, the earliest dawn of awareness of God's will, the earliest slight, passing conviction that we may have failed God. All imply some tendency toward life, some measure of salvation, the beginning of a deliverance from a blind, unfeeling heart that has remained insensible to God.

(2) The path to salvation continues by the power of convincing or convicting grace, that is, repentance, which brings us a larger measure of self-knowledge, and a farther deliverance from having a heart of stone.

In time we experience the full measure of Christian salvation, in which "by his grace" we are "saved, through trusting him" (Eph. 2:8). This consists of two fundamental branches: justification and sanctification.

(3) By justifying grace, or justification, we are saved from the guilt of sin and restored to the favor of God.

(4) By fulfilling grace, or sanctification, we are saved from the power and root of sin and restored to the image of God.

2. Both Instantaneously and Gradually

Experience as well as Scripture shows that this salvation is both instantaneous and gradual. It begins the moment we are justified by the holy, humble, gentle, patient love of God toward us which calls us to love others. It gradually increases from that moment, like a grain of "mustard-seed, which is smaller than any seed in the ground at its sowing" (Mark 4:31), but afterwards puts forth large branches and in time becomes a great tree. Finally, at some point the heart is cleansed from all sin and filled with pure love for God and neighbor. But even that abundant love increases, until we "fully grow up into Christ" and at last attain to maturity, "measured by nothing less than the full stature of Christ" (Eph. 4:13, 15).

But how are we to work out this salvation? The Apostle answers, "with fear and trembling." The same phrase occurs in the letter to the Ephesians in connection with a different analogy, where servants are called to follow the instructions of those to whom they are accountable "with fear and trembling." Obviously, this is a metaphor that is not to be taken literally—for who would wish to see someone visibly trembling and quaking? But what follows illuminates the meaning: They are to serve "singlemindedly, as serving Christ. Do not offer merely the outward show of service, to curry favour," but as servants of Christ (Eph. 6:5, 6). These strong expressions imply two things: First, that everything be done with the utmost earnestness of spirit and with all care and caution; and second, that they be done with the utmost diligence, speed, punctuality, and exactness. By analogy, we transfer this image to the task of working out to completion our own salvation. With this same temper and manner, let us work to serve God with earnestness and diligence.

3.   In Practice

What practical steps can we take toward these ends? The prophet Isaiah gives us the right general direction for our crucial first steps: "Cease to do evil and learn to do right" (Isa. 1:17). If you ever desire that God should elicit in you that trust in him out of which comes both present and future salvation by grace, first you must turn your back on the life of sin. Avoid every evil word and work. Abstain even from the appearance of evil. Having done this, then you are ready to "learn to do right." That implies becoming energetic in good works, both works of prayer as well as works of mercy. Learn how to pray both in common worship and in secret. Fast in secret, "and your Father who sees what is secret will give you your reward" (Matt. 6:18). "Search the scriptures" (John 5:39). Hear them in public, read them in private, meditate deeply upon them. At every opportunity, be a partaker of the Lord's Supper. Do this in remembrance of Christ and he will meet you at his own table.

Let your conversation be imbued with "saltness" (Matt. 5:13), interesting and preserving, among the children of God. Insofar as it is possible, do good to everyone you meet, both to their bodies and their souls. "Stand firm and immovable, and work for the Lord always" (1 Cor. 15:58). Deny yourselves and take up your cross daily. Avoid any temporal enticement that does not prepare you for taking pleasure in God. Willingly embrace every means of drawing near to God, even though it be a cross, difficult for flesh and blood. Having this redemption in Christ, "let us advance toward maturity" (Heb. 6:3) until "we walk in the light as he himself is in the light" (1 John 1:7), enabled to say honestly that God is faithful and just not only to forgive our sins, but to "cleanse" us from "every kind of wrong" (1 John 1:9).

"Therefore": The Connecting Link Between God's Work and Ours

Some will doubt that there is any clear connection between God's work and our work. Some imagine a flat opposition between them. Some will ask: If it is God that works in us both to will and to do, why do we also need to be working? Does not God's work supersede the necessity of our working at all? Furthermore, does it not render our working useless as well as superfluous? If God does everything, what is left for us to do?

So our natural reasoning prematurely concludes, and at first hearing it seems quite plausible. But, as we will see when we consider the connection more deeply, there is no logical inconsistency or opposition between God's acting and our acting. Rather there is a subtle interweaving, in our text, of these two intrinsically correlated themes: (1) God works, therefore we *can* work; and (2) God works, therefore we *must* work.

1. God Works in Us; Therefore We Can Work

God works in us, therefore we can work. Otherwise, it would be impossible. If God did not work, it would be impossible for us to work toward fulfilling our salvation. "Then who can be saved?" the disciples asked. "Jesus looked at them, and said, 'For men this is impossible; but everything is possible for God.' " (Matt. 19:25, 26). If God does not work in us, salvation is quite impossible for anyone, any finite person, born of flesh and blood. For the whole course of human history is not merely sick, but, to use the Apostle's term, "dead in sins and wickedness" (Eph. 2:1). It is not possible for the dead to do anything on their own behalf unless God should raise them from the dead. It was not possible for Lazarus to begin to rise from the grave until the Lord gave him life. It is equally impossible for us to rise up out of our sins or to make even the slightest motion toward it until the One who has all power over heaven and earth calls our deadened souls into life.

Yet this must not be used as an excuse for us to continue to sin and blame God for our condition, or say despairingly: "Only God can do anything for us, we can do nothing." Even if we admit that all souls are spiritually deadened through sin by nature, this cannot excuse us, for no one exists purely in a fallen state without grace in any form. There is none of us, unless we imagine that someone has the power absolutely to quench the Spirit, who is finally alienated from the grace of God. None of us is entirely destitute of what is sometimes called "natural conscience," but which is better called preceding (or prevenient) grace. Each of us has some greater or lesser measure of this. It does not wait on us to call it forth. Each of us, sooner or later, has some faint breath of wholesome desire, although it is common for us to stifle it before it can find much deep rootage or produce much fruit. Each of us has some measure of that light, some faint glimmering ray, which sooner or later, more or less, enlightens everyone that comes into the world (John 1:9). Each of us, except those of that small number whose conscience is virtually burnt out, feels more or less uneasy in acting contrary to the light of conscience. Therefore, we do not sin because we have no grace whatever, but rather because we do not use the grace we have.

On this basis, precisely because God is working in us, we are now able to work to fulfill God's saving purpose. Since God works in us "for his own chosen purpose," without any merit of our own, both in our willing and doing, it is possible for us to live out our life in full accountability to God. It is possible for us to "love because he loved us first" (1 John 4:19) and to "live in love as Christ loved you" (Eph. 5:2). We know that Jesus was speaking truly when he said: "Apart from me you can do nothing" (John 15:5). But at the same time every believer has "strength for anything through him who gives me power" (Phil. 4:13).

God has joined these two complementary aspects together in the experience of every genuine believer. We must take care never to separate them. Beware of that mock humility that pleads as an excuse for willful disobedience, "O I can do nothing!" and stops there, without speaking of grace active in love. Think twice, I beg of you. For if we can really do nothing, then we cannot exercise faith, a miserable condition and hardly a mature salvation. Surely it is not so. We *can* do something through Christ who strengthens us. Let us stir up the spark of grace that is now in us, and God will give us more.

2. God Works in Us; Therefore We *Must* Work

"Sharing in God's work, we urge this appeal upon you: you have received the grace of God; do not let it go for nothing" (2 Cor. 6:1, 2). These are the very words of the Apostle. If we do not share in God's working in us, then God may in some ways cease his work. Note carefully the general rule by which God's gracious giving invariably proceeds: One who "has will be given more"; one who "has not"—who does improve on the grace already given—"will forfeit even what he has" (Mark 4:25). Even St. Augustine, who was supposed by some to favor the contrary teaching, made the remark: "He who made us without ourselves will not save us without ourselves." God will not save us unless we listen to the Apostle: " 'Save yourselves,' he said, 'from this crooked age' " (Acts 2:40). God will not save those who refuse to "run the great race of faith and take hold of eternal life" (1 Tim. 6:12). Unless you "struggle to get in through the narrow door" (Luke 13:24), "leave self behind," take up the cross, and "come with me" (Mark 8:34), you will miss God's saving action. Do not expect God to do your part for you. "All the more then, my friends, exert yourselves to clinch God's choice and calling of you" (2 Pet. 1–10).

"You must work," Jesus said, "not for this perishable food, but for the food that lasts, the food of eternal life" (John 6:27). We can say with Jesus, though in a different sense, "My Father has never yet ceased his work, and I am working too" (John 5:17). The remembrance that God works ceaselessly in us helps us to "never tire of doing good" (Gal. 6:9).

By the grace of God which goes before us, accompanies us and follows us, continue steadily in the work of faith, in the patience of hope, and the labor of love (1 Thess. 1:3). "Stand firm and immovable, and work for the Lord always, work without limit, since you know that in the Lord your labour cannot be lost" (1 Cor. 15:58). "May the God of peace, who brought up from the dead our Lord Jesus, the great Shepherd of the sheep, by the blood of the eternal covenant, make you perfect in all goodness so that you may do his will; and may he make of us what he would have us be through Jesus Christ, to whom be glory for ever and ever! Amen." (Heb. 13:20, 21).

Deliver me, O God, from too intense an application to even necessary business. I know how this dissipates my thoughts from the one central purpose of all my business, and impairs that lively awareness that I would have of thee always at hand. I know the narrowness of my heart, and that excessive attention to earthly things leaves no room for thee. O teach me to go through all my employments with so truly disengaged a heart, that I may still see thee in all things, and see thee as continually looking upon me and searching my soul; that I may never impair that liberty of spirit which is necessary for the love of thee. Amen. (*WJW* XI, 207)

O for a thousand tongues to sing
My great Redeemer's praise,
The glories of my God and King,
The triumphs of His grace!

My gracious Master and my God,
Assist me to proclaim,
To spread through all the earth abroad
The honors of Thy name.

Jesus! the name that charms our fears,
That bids our sorrows cease;
'Tis music in the sinner's ears;
'Tis life, and health, and peace.

He breaks the pow'r of cancelled sin;
He sets the pris'ner free.
His blood can make the foulest clean;
His blood availed for me.

He speaks and, listening to His voice,
New life the dead receive.
The mournful, broken hearts rejoice;
The humble poor believe.

Hear Him, ye deaf; His praise, ye dumb,
Your loosen'd tongues employ;
Ye blind, behold your Saviour come;
And leap, ye lame, for joy.

(WH 1)

ABBREVIATIONS

WH   *Wesley Hymnbook,* ed. Franz Hildebrandt (Kansas City, Mo.: Lillenas, 1962).

WJW   *The Works of John Wesley,* ed. Thomas Jackson, 3rd ed. 1831, vols. I–XIV (London: Wesleyan Conference Office, 1872). Original texts of the five sermons are found in Vol. V, 87ff., 98ff., 212ff., and Vol. VI, 65ff., 506ff. The prayers of John Wesley are adapted from "A Collection of Forms of Prayer for Every Day in the Week," "A Collection of Prayers for Families," and "Prayers for Children" (Vol. XI, 203–72).